STOP
THE FOOLISHNESS
FOR WIVES

A Practical Guide
to a Healthy Marriage

FIONA ARTHURS

STOP
THE FOOLISHNESS
FOR WIVES

A Practical Guide to a Healthy Marriage

Revised Edition: 2019
Stop the Foolishness for Wives: A Practical Guide to a Healthy Marriage / Fiona Arthurs
Paperback ISBN: 978-1-946453-73-0
eBook ISBN: 978-1-946453-74-7

CONTENTS

Words of Praise for *Stop the Foolishness* 5

Dedication 7

Acknowledgments 9

Is It All On Me? 13

Too Weak to Fight...17

The 'Tude 22

Can I Exchange My Gift? 29

The Nagger...33

The Grudge-Holder..37

Minefield..42

"The Look"...47

Concealed Weapon...51

I Can Do It Better 57

The Mother Syndrome 60

I'm Not Into What He's Into...64

But I Have Needs Too! 69

What About the Joneses? 76

Stupid Feminism...79

What About the Children? 82

Childhood Baggage 85

The Socks Are On the Floor Again 91

Social-Media Trap 95

Keeping Up Appearances..98

Not Tonight, Dear...101

In-Law Interference..109

Where's the Wife?..112

The Journey Continues...118

Foolishness Assessment...120

WORDS OF PRAISE FOR *STOP THE FOOLISHNESS*

DeeDee Freeman, author of *Focus: It's the Promise Not the Process That Matters*, writes:

Having been married for over thirty years, I've personally experienced the challenges intended to destroy relationships. By virtue of entering the God-ordained covenant of marriage, it is inevitable that there will be obstacles to overcome. However, the good news for us as believers is—WE ALWAYS WIN! Through understanding, discipline and consistent application of the Word of God, you can experience God's best by enjoying a marriage that reflects God's best.

Ministering to multitudes of women, I have witnessed how we as wives have the potential to cooperate with the enemy in destroying our marriages, leading to the demise of our family. It is important that we become ambassadors of healthy, thriving marriages, making this covenant attractive. By honoring our roles as wives, we will begin to seek God for direction, thus building foundations that will last for generations to come. In Stop the Foolishness, Fiona uses a combination of compelling Scripture, empathetic anecdotes and practical takeaways to guide you into becoming a wife that both God and your husband are pleased with. I'm thankful for resources like this, as I wish I'd had access to such wisdom at the beginning of my relationship. Yet, no matter how many years you have been married, increase is always available. I'm living proof that you can have the marriage of your dreams by simply committing to have better.

I admonish you to read this book with careful introspection, examining yourself and allowing the Holy Spirit to highlight areas in which you can improve. When you're done, share it with other wives so that marriages can benefit from the wisdom God has given Fiona as shared here.

Pat Ashley, author of *Marriage Is a Blessing*, writes:

Fiona's book is a must read for every woman, married or single. It is a powerful tool full of godly instructions given in a clear and practical way.

This book is a must read if you want to be a wise woman who will build her house and marriage in a way that honors God. I highly recommend Stop the Foolishness as a go-to guide for every woman who is ready for a healthy relationship with her husband.

DEDICATION

To my best friend, Paul Arthurs, who has endured the lows and enjoyed the highs of my journey to wisdom. Though I am still a work in progress, Paul, you have been patient, kept no record of wrongs (phew!), and loved me both in my foolishness and wisdom. I am eternally grateful to God for you. In the words of one song title, "Life Is Better with You." I love you.

To my daughters, Lydia and Sophia: I pray you can avoid some of the mistakes your mother made and learn early in life, and certainly in your marriages, to be that wise woman who builds her house.

To my son, Carlton: When the time is right, may you find a wise woman who will build her home.

ACKNOWLEDGMENTS

To my parents, Drs. Ezekiel and Eunor Guti: What can I say? I am who I am because of you. Dad, you always showed us how a man of God treats his wife. Mum, you showed us nothing but the respect, love, and admiration you have for Dad. You are truly an example of a wise woman who builds her home. The words of the song "You Raise Me Up" ring true when I think of you both. You have always seen the best in me and push me toward God's purpose for my life.

To my parents-in-law, Pastors Carlton and Sheila Arthurs, and Arthurs family in-laws: Thank you for accepting me into the family and treating me as one of your own. I am so thankful I don't have to deal with "in-law issues."

To the Guti Girls: You have always encouraged me and called forth those things in me I didn't always see. You are great cheerleaders, intercessors, and encouragers. So thankful that God put us together. Guti Girls Forever!

To all those who edited the book and provided material for examples: Thank you!

INTRODUCTION

> *A wise woman builds her home, but a foolish woman*
> *tears it down with her own hands.*
> **Proverbs 14:1 NLT**

> *A wise woman strengthens and helps to build her*
> *marriage, but a foolish woman messes up her marriage*
> *using her own hands.*
> **(Fiona's paraphrase)**

The words of Proverbs 14:1 have been read, heard, and proclaimed many times. But what do they mean in a practical way? How does a wise woman "build her house"? How does a foolish one tear it down "with her own hands"? How is she able to destroy her own home? To understand the difference between the wise and foolish women in this verse, first let's consider how the foolish woman tears down her house. If we are aware of what the foolish woman does to tear down her house, or mess up her marriage, we can certainly work to avoid those pitfalls and work toward building up, which will bring us to our desired destination: a godly, peaceful, loving home. As this is a book for wives, we understand that a strong, godly marriage is the foundation for a godly home. I have found that as wives, it's not that we don't know what to do, but in between the doing, we unknowingly tear down our homes. Knowing what tearing down looks like will help shed light on our actions and reveal areas of growth.

I believe the Lord urged me to write this book to help both me and others to have the marriages and homes He desires for us. I do not write because I have arrived or achieved total wisdom, but because God has burdened my heart to encourage other women to walk together on this journey. It is not easy, but God gives us the grace to do what He asks us to do if we obey His Word.

I mainly write from personal experience of my ongoing, lifelong journey to becoming a wise woman, but I'll also share stories of women I've encountered along the way. The information shared is not exhaustive, but it is a tool for the everyday woman seeking to be wise.

This book is for the woman who desires a happy and successful marriage in the Lord. It is for the woman who sees the marriage she dreamed of slowly slipping away and who wants to gain insight to bring God's wisdom into action to turn things around. It is for the woman who is about to embark on the journey of holy matrimony and wants to avoid the pitfalls many women fall into. It is for the divorced woman who wants to remarry and avoid past mistakes. It is also for every older woman who mentors younger women, "that they may teach the young women to be sober, to love their husbands, to love their children" (Titus 2:4 KJV).

If you are in an abusive marriage, this book is not for you. There are many resources and programs for women in domestic-violence situations. The information in this book will not help you. Seek help immediately.

The first edition of this book was titled Foolish Things Wives Do to Mess Up Their Marriages. The response from both men and women has been very positive, and my husband Paul and I realized we should have a companion book, Stop the Foolishness for Husbands. So Paul wrote the men's edition so we can all learn how to Stop the Foolishness!

Most of the book remains largely unchanged as I believe that if it works, then don't mess with it. Here is some of the feedback that I have received: "I felt like you were a fly on the wall in my house!" "I thought I was the only one who dealt with those issues!" "My husband shared that he noticed a change in my attitude toward him and our marriage is now healthy!" "Thank you for writing this book. I didn't realize that I was tearing down my house. I have made some changes and since then I have started enjoying my marriage."

For this new edition, I have added a "Foolishness Assessment" for you to use before and after reading the book. You should definitely see some growth. I have also updated several chapters with additional info. You will find some conversation helpers because often you know you should say something the right way but lack the skills in knowing what to say. I give examples of what you can say, but feel free to use your own words.

I encourage you to read this book prayerfully and listen to the voice of the Holy Spirit, who will lead you on your journey to wisdom.

CHAPTER 1

IS IT ALL ON ME?

*A wise woman builds her home, but a foolish woman
tears it down with her own hands.*
Proverbs 14:1 NLT

Proverbs 14:1 tells us that we as women, not our husbands, are the builders of our homes. Have you ever wondered why God did not say "a wise *man* builds his house"? After all, the husband is the head of the wife and the leader of the family. It would seem that the weight of building the home should be on him. But in His infinite wisdom, God puts the stability of the home on the wife.

We were formed in the image and likeness of God (Genesis 1:27). Most importantly, God made the woman to be a "helper" or great influence for her husband (Genesis 2:18). This influence was intended to be used to build and pattern a marriage after God's desires for marriage and family.

Throughout the Bible, God shows us how He wants our marriages to be (Proverbs 18:22; 1 Corinthians 11:9; Ephesians 5:22, 25). He wants us to build our marriages and homes in that God-like image. You and I, as wise women, are to use the godly influence we have to build our homes. Not to manipulate, but to build. Not to abuse, but to build. Not to tear down, but to build. I often tell women to stop crying over their marriages and use the influence God endowed them with and build their home. Dear wife, your influence is so strong that you have to be careful not to abuse it. Unfortunately, most of us never learn how to use that influence but instead cry foul every other day.

God did not say a wise man builds his house, but a wise woman does. She holds influence. I believe my husband is the architect and designer of our home, but as a woman, I must then take the blueprint and build my home. The power of a woman is unfathomable. Have you noticed how you, as the woman, can control the atmosphere in your home? In my own house, I have found that when I am frustrated and on blast with instructions to the children (and even my husband), the house is tense. I have also found that instead of the children obeying quickly, as I would expect when I'm bellowing instructions in a serious tone, they actually move more slowly and bicker among themselves. Everyone in the house becomes agitated because Mommy is agitated. As a mother and wife, I have the power to bring peace to my home or put stress on my family.

God expects me to build my house, and He has given me every-thing I need to build a solid, unshakable home.

If I am the one to build the house, I must come to terms with the fact that any existing problems in my home are not only my husband's fault (ouch!). As women, it is easy for us to blame our husbands for anything that goes wrong in the home:

> "He's not taking leadership."
> "He's lazy and shiftless."
> "He lacks initiative."
> "He's bad with money."
> "He doesn't take spiritual leadership in the home."
> "He doesn't help me in the house."

And the list goes on.

All of these could be true, but I daresay your husband is not the sole cause of problems in the home. Many are caused by us women. Yes, I said it! We play a large role in the dysfunction in our home. It is with the fool-ish woman's own hands that she tears down her house. She is responsible for her actions. She cannot blame her husband.

Wow, it's scary to know we must own our actions! No matter how you may feel your husband drives you to your poor actions and reactions, you play a significant role in many of the negative interactions that take place within the home.

Let's review 1 Peter 2:12 and 3:1 (NKJV):

> *Having your conduct honorable among the Gentiles, that when they speak against you as evildoers, they may, by your good works which they observe, glorify God in the day of visitation.*
>
> *Wives, likewise, be submissive to your own husbands, that even if some do not obey the word, they, without a word, may be won by the conduct of their wives.*

These Scriptures show us how powerful we are. We are creatures of influence. We don't even have to use words to influence, but our actions can yield positive results.

Proverbs 14:1b says a foolish woman tears her home down with her own hands. At first she set out to build her home, but somewhere along the way she began to take it down one brick at a time, plucking it down piece by piece. I imagine that when she was first married, she was likely determined to not be like her mother. She watched how poorly her mother treated her father and vowed to never be like that. She took the teachings from church and applied them, but then she grew weary. She has been doing all the right things—at least she thinks so—and doesn't see any change. She has been rising early to pray and stand in the gap for her home, but things don't seem to be changing much, and she has grown frustrated. Now she is beginning to unknowingly tear down her home with her own hands. Maybe she wasn't necessarily frustrated, but she just began to take her husband for granted; she became complacent and unknowingly began to tear down the very thing that she had worked hard to build. It's the little things she does that destroy her home—her attitude toward her husband, the way she neglects her wifely duties, her tongue, how she allows her family to interfere in her marriage.

I believe the phrase "her own hands" refers to her actions. It is our actions, both verbal and nonverbal, that we use to tear down our homes. We are creatures of influence, and our actions will either build our homes or place a time bomb under them. Not only does "her own hands" refer to her actions, but "her own hands" means that she can't blame someone else for what is going on in her home. It's "her own hands"—my own hands that destroy my home. The enemy that is destroying her home is not outside but within her. The greatest enemy to the health of your marriage is not your husband; the greatest enemy is within you. My dear sister, you hold the power in your hands (actions) to have a healthy and successful marriage.

The following chapters discuss ways foolish women tear down their homes and marriages. The list is by no means exhaustive but is made up of things I've come across in my over twenty years of marriage and of talking to women. As you read, I believe the Holy Spirit is going to do a work from within to make us wise women who build up, instead of mess up, our marriages. Remember you hold the power within you to build your home.

DISCUSSION QUESTIONS

1. What are the strengths in your marriage?

2. Where does your marriage struggle?

3. What areas in your marriage do you take responsibility for?

4. What are your hopes for reading this book?

CHAPTER 2

TOO WEAK TO FIGHT

For You have armed me with strength for the battle.
Psalm 18:39a NKJV

I have found that marriage and parenting bring out the best or the worst in us. I believe God designed our homes to be a place where His Word is fleshed out, where we are to live it out. I strongly believe God gives us spouses, children, and family members to work out the fruit of the Spirit in us. Areas in my character where I thought I was mature are constantly challenged, which is good for me because until Christ is fully formed in us (Galatians 4:19), we are falling short and need to keep growing. It's easy to be kind to other people and their children, but we're often impatient with our own. I'm glad there are no hidden cameras in my house where people could see me lose it—especially with my kids. Often the root of my struggle is in not having spent the time I need in His presence each morning. This is where I exchange my strength for His, where I get a heart transplant so I can have His heart, and where I put on the whole armor of God as Ephesians 6:10–18 tells me (and as my husband's mother encourages the ladies at our church to do daily).

I need the armor because I'll face battles I cannot fight in the flesh. Often we are fighting spiritual battles in the flesh, and this is usually a result of not spending time on our knees. Your husband is not your enemy, though Satan would love for you to believe so. Our eyes can only be opened to the real enemy when we spend time in His presence.

> *For our struggle is not against flesh and blood, but against the rulers, against the authorities, against the powers of this dark world and against the spiritual forces of evil in the heavenly realms.*
> **Ephesians 6:12 NIV**

We need to derive strength from God's Word and seek His presence daily in order to deal with our husbands and children. We need His strength to walk in the fruit of the Spirit. The time spent on my knees with the Lord is when I learn to walk in the Spirit. This helps me not fulfill the lusts of the flesh, not to speak what comes to my mind to my husband and children, not to react in the flesh and speak hurtful words when frustrated. Instead I choose to be quiet (even though I could easily defend myself), to gain strength to be quiet (even when I can easily articulate and run circles around my husband with my words), to not cut my husband down to size (with just a few well-put-together words or "the look"). When we have a personal, intimate relationship with the Lord, we are able to walk in the Spirit. I cannot walk in the Spirit if I have not stepped into the spirit world and commanded my day. As a wife, you may be operating in a spirit that is not the Holy Spirit.

While traveling through the Hartsfield Atlanta Airport, I noticed a quote that resonated with me:

"My plan of operation must depend on that of the enemy."
**GENERAL JOSEPH E. JOHNSTON, 1864
(AMERICAN CIVIL WAR)**

I know the enemy comes to steal, kill, and destroy. Therefore, I must plan my offense and defense through my intimate time with God. I must be sober and vigilant because the enemy is always seeking an opportunity to destroy my home. Never put your guard down when you are married; the enemy will try every possible tactic to ruin your home or to use you to tear it down.

I must always be aware of my enemy and plan my operation and battle plan accordingly.

BENEFITS OF KNEE TIME

1. **Revealed secrets.** (Psalm 25:14, 119:98) God can show what is going on with your husband even if he hasn't told you, and you can begin to pray. Maybe something is going on at work, or temptation is lurking at the doorstep. Run interference against the enemy by keeping your appointment with God.

2. **Strength derived to make it through the day.** (Matthew 6:33, 1 Peter 5:7, Psalm 18:39) Every wife needs to take time to gain strength for the daily tasks she has to complete and for the constant demands on her.

3. **Your character becomes more like God.** We tend to pick up the character traits of people with whom we have intimacy (Galatians 5:22–25). Paul and I have become very much alike because we are intimate. I have picked up many of his habits and vice versa. Thus, when we continue to develop our intimacy with God, we become more and more like Him.

4. **Changed attitude toward your spouse.** I intentionally didn't say "your spouse changes," though that can be a benefit. Sometimes the spouse never changes, but if your attitude does, you can face whatever challenges come your way. When the Holy Spirit begins to work on us as a result of being in His presence, we are left with no excuse for bad attitudes, unforgiveness, grudges, etc. When I'm tempted to retaliate, I find I don't have the strength or even the desire to do so because I have been changed in His presence. Christ has been formed in me through prayer. He has taken over my reactions and responses.

A word of caution: do not make the mistake of thinking because you are spending time in God's presence, you are now the spiritual head. A foolish woman usurps spiritual authority because she "hears from God" and uses that to manipulate her husband. Use wisdom in sharing with your husband what God is speaking to you. Ask Him to show your husband what you are seeing, and you'll be surprised when your husband says the exact thing you heard from God.

KNOW WHOM TO RUN TO

As part of our ministry to women in my church, we hold a prayer boot camp where we women spend a night away from home (in a hotel) to seek God's face and allow Him to work in us and reveal to us where we need to grow. It is a time of sweet fellowship with the Holy Spirit and with sisters in Christ. One particular year, I was dealing with a lot of stresses and frankly didn't want to even be at the boot camp. I kept wishing the weekend would come and go just so I could go back to nursing my wounds. I had quite a pity party going with all the trimmings. I usually go to the hotel the night before, just to settle down and prepare myself for the camp as a leader. My husband, Paul, picked me up from work to take me to the hotel. I was very quiet and spoke little on the way there. I wasn't upset, but plain sad. Just feeling depressed and in some ways hopeless about certain things in my life that hadn't been moving as I had hoped, prayed, and fasted for.

As a man in tune with his wife, Paul asked me what was wrong. *Well!* Everything in me wanted to emotionally vomit all my stuff, leaving him to clean up the mess. Normally I'd have gone into all the things wrong in my life and also scold him for things he didn't know but I thought he should do something about. I basically would've projected my negative feelings onto him and made him feel less. Instead I just said, "This is something I need to work out with God. I need to pray this through." Thankfully, Paul didn't ask for details or press the issue.

After he left, I lay on the bed and cried. I didn't need to be strong for anyone, so it flowed like a river. After, I read our boot camp theme verse, Hebrews 11:35a. Then I went to 1 Kings 17:8–24 and 2 Kings 4:8–43 to read of the women who received their dead raised to life. As I read and re-read these women's stories, something in me rose up, and I began to speak life into the dead things that were tormenting me. Read about the widow of Zarephath and the Shunamite woman. Something about that Shunamite lady baffles me. Now, I have three kids—two daughters and a son. God help me if something happens to any of them, and God *really* help if something was to happen to the one son. This woman simply put her dead son on the prophet Elisha's bed and went to find him. When her husband asked why she needed to make an unplanned trip, she simply answered, "It is well." Study the caliber of women who received their dead raised to life. We can learn from the Shunamite woman. She knew when to run to God. She knew what she needed could only come from Him. A foolish woman tries to get her husband to fulfill her and to work miracles. A wise woman knows when to run to God and ask Him to give her the desires of her heart.

When you have a personal relationship with the Lord and spend time on your knees, you know there are some things your husband can handle and other things only God can. Know the difference. When I look back on that one evening, I'm so thankful I didn't unload on my poor husband but instead went to my Father. To Jesus, the lover of my soul. The One who could fix it, make it all better. Run to Jesus, dear sister, and stop demanding your husband fill the void that only God can.

DO YOU BUILD UP OR TEAR DOWN?
A foolish woman neglects her knee time, but a wise woman spends intimate time with her Heavenly Father and is empowered by Him.

DISCUSSION QUESTIONS

1. What is your plan for setting aside time with the Lord?

2. How does better understanding the enemy's schemes motivate your prayers?

3. Which benefit of intimacy with God listed is most appealing to you? Why?

CHAPTER 3

THE 'TUDE

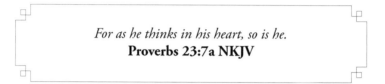

For as he thinks in his heart, so is he.
Proverbs 23:7a NKJV

I was watching TV with my kids as I attempted to braid their hair (*attempted* being the operative word), and I heard one girl tell her friend, who had a bad attitude, to "drop the 'tude." We as women have to drop the 'tude toward our relationships because it's destroying our homes.

I am convinced that attitude is everything.

What a woman thinks in her heart about her husband, he becomes in her mind. Our attitude determines whether we are building up or tearing down. Our attitude is related to the joy and peace we experience in our relationships. The state of your marriage is largely due to your attitude toward your relationship and your husband. A wise woman builds her house by the happy anticipation and joy she has toward her relationship. A foolish woman tears it down with her negative attitude. We have to drop the 'tude.

In 2010, I'd just returned from Zimbabwe and had to attend a women's conference at the Wheaton Christian Center the next night. I arrived home on a Tuesday morning and had to be at the event the next evening. Jetlagged, I asked Paul to drive me to the conference site. He initially said no, but he later agreed. I copped an attitude because he had dared to tell me no! It was our first evening together, and I was already having an attitude. I had the opportunity to make a conscious decision to drop the 'tude before ruining the precious time with my husband.

Maybe you have allowed the thought to linger that your marriage was a mistake and you want out. Or maybe you've decided you'll never be happy with this man and resigned yourself to a life of misery. These attitudes can cause you to not see anything good in your mate. In a sense, you begin to despise him. When he touches you, your skin crawls and you stiffen because he no longer pleases you. Do you ever wonder why you can't give yourself to him anymore? You dread his caresses. You find every excuse not to have sex with him, even though you desire it. You've let evil thoughts linger in your mind, and now you see your husband, and everything he does, through a negative lens. We must not let negative thoughts linger, because they indeed affect our attitude toward our husbands.

I remember having a hard time with my attitude toward my husband. At the time, I felt he wasn't measuring up to the picture of the man of God I thought I'd married. I felt he wasn't helping enough around the house. I felt I was doing everything to keep our home together, and if it weren't for me, everything would crumble.

Isn't it amazing how, as women, we think of ourselves more highly than we ought? We start to think we are better than our husbands and can lead the family better. It's amazing how our thoughts can lead us astray, even to the point of leaving our husbands. I once heard a woman say she had "outgrown" her husband, so she left him. How do you "outgrow" your husband, if not because of your attitude that you are now better than him and can do without him?

We have to be careful what we allow people to say about our husbands; it's easy to internalize those words and begin to view our mates in a negative light. Be careful whom you confide in. Be careful of girlfriends who will take your side and vilify your husband. Be careful of well-meaning friends or male coworkers who tell you how you are missing out by remaining committed to your husband.

My negative attitude toward my husband was fostered through conversations with people who cared about and wanted the best for him, but it was slowly killing my love for him. My attitude was growing increasingly negative. My hope had been deferred, and now my heart was sick (Proverbs 13:12). I *thought* my *hope* had been deferred, but really, my *common sense* had been. Don't let people speak into your heart words that will change your heart about your mate. Sometimes we don't realize what's happening until it's almost too late. That is what happened to me. The negative seed was slowly growing, but I didn't know it until the Holy Spirit shook me to my core in my quiet time. Hence, the vital importance of quiet time where the Holy Spirit works in us.

Right around our ten-year anniversary, my attitude toward my husband had grown so bad I knew I had to change before I acted out my thoughts—which were influenced by what others had said. Paul's negative traits consumed my thoughts. I began to see everything negative he did and overlooked all the good things about him. My gaze was fixed on the negatives, which looked like an insurmountable mountain. I began to believe he took me for granted and did not care about me or love me as much as he said. If he didn't daily say how much he loved me, I'd assume I was no longer important to him. Things had become so bad in my mind that we needed quick intervention. I began to communicate that we were headed for disaster if we didn't do something quickly.

The truth was, I needed intervention; it was more about me than him. For our anniversary, I convinced Paul to attend a marriage conference with me. It was a good idea, but my reasoning was flawed. I felt he needed to hear something that would help him become the man I wanted to be married to. But it was I who needed to hear how to be a wife after God's own heart, a wife whose heart her husband securely trusts. I thank God for giving me enough sense to run for help, rather than let the negativity fester and cause me to act out of my flesh or frustration.

Have you ever looked at a food package and noticed, next to the large picture, this disclaimer: "Not actual size"? Or maybe when looking at a product online, you clicked "enlarge" to see more detail? Well, I'd clicked "enlarge" on my marriage and was stuck there. I was focused on the negatives. If you look at the negatives through a magnifying glass, you'll always find plenty of small things—that suddenly seem much larger than they really are.

Again, beware what you allow others to speak into your heart. A girlfriend may highlight a negative trait about your spouse, and suddenly you begin to notice annoying habits you hadn't even thought about before. Don't let your attitude toward your husband become tempted to negativity. As the hymn goes, "Oh, be careful, little ears, what you hear."

Our poor attitude is due to letting unproductive thoughts move about freely in our minds. We must cast down arguments and every high thing that exalts itself against the knowledge of God, by bringing every thought into captivity to the obedience of Christ (2 Corinthians 10:5). We must cast down every negative word spoken over our mates and every negative thought that comes to our minds.

An excerpt from and adaptation of a blog I found impactful (Proverbs14verse1.blogspot.com)…[1]

> We must filter everything through God's Word, purposefully and diligently rebuking every thought that is not compatible with His Word. Ladies, this means not entertaining even the most fleeting of thoughts that might be out of line. We must understand

we are fighting a battle for our families. Satan wants to steal, kill and destroy, and he wants your family. We must be on guard with something so important as our thought-life. He knows if he can destroy the heart of the home, the rest will come crashing down.

Taking thoughts captive is not easy. Just as a soldier might take an enemy hostage, conflict is involved. The soul is warring with the mind—the Word of God vs. man's sinfulness. We must actively chase after wrong thinking, take it captive and ensure it is not allowed freedom to destroy. From the very beginning when that seed is small, the small lie whispers in our minds, we must rebuke it. But more than that—we must combat it with Scripture and follow up with action if appropriate. Here are some examples:

Unproductive Thought: I have too much on my plate; I can't handle all the pressure.

Biblical Thought: With God all things are possible (Matthew 19:26). I can do all things through Him who strengthens me (Isaiah 41:10). What He wants me to get done today will get done, even if it's not what was on my list.

Follow-Up Actions: Use a time-management tool or list to help manage your tasks. See what needs to come off your plate so you can be more present both physically and emotionally. Ask for help. Most times, we have not because we ask not.

Unproductive Thought: Nobody helps me around here. I do all the work while everyone lies around doing nothing.

Biblical Thought: The Lord is my helper. I rely on Him for strength. Love is patient, love is kind (1 Corinthians 13:4). Help me show the light of Christ and be kind to those who might not be helping. Jesus came first to serve, not be served; help me to serve in my home like He did to the world (Ephesians 6:7).

Follow-Up Actions: Don't be a Martha and get angry at Mary. Ask for help. Don't assume everyone sees you working. Make a chore chart so the family knows their responsibilities. If things still aren't working, have a family meeting or stop doing everything. As long as you do it, why should they?

Unproductive Thought: I could have handled this situation much better than my husband did. He really messed things up. He always makes poor decisions.

Biblical Thought: Love is not proud, not rude, not self-seeking, not easily angered. It always protects, always trusts, always hopes, always perseveres (1 Corinthians 13:4, 5, 7). God wants me to be patient with my husband as he leads, even when he makes a wrong decision. Instead of blaming or being angry, I'll use this time to pray for him instead. I understand he is responsible to God for his leading, just as I am responsible for my response and my actions.

Follow-Up Actions: Pray for him. When the time is right, bring up the situation in an effort to gain understanding, but do not attack him. What you hear may surprise you. Use your influence to make it important to him to seek your advice before making a decision.

Unproductive Thought: My husband doesn't talk to me. He'd rather sit like a dud and watch the game every night.

Biblical Thought: Love always trusts and assumes the best (1 Corinthians 13:4). I should not assume he is being spiteful or evil. Maybe he's tired when he gets home. I don't know what happened at work or what he is going through. Lord, help me to be discerning and show me what he is dealing with.

Follow-Up Actions: Do a self-evaluation. Are you pleasant to be around, or are you always nagging and nitpicking? Find a way to communicate your desire to be with him without complaining. "I really enjoy spending time with you and look forward to the moments we spend together. It fills my love tank. When can we schedule our time alone?"

This also applies to all who have children. Don't let other people cause you to think your kids are evil and there's nothing good in them. I'm not saying to bury your head in the sand and ignore bad behavior, but start to look for the good in your children. Philemon verse 6 (NKJV) says, "That the sharing of your faith may become effective by the acknowledgment of every good thing which is in you in Christ Jesus."

This verse reminds us to communicate the good. Address the bad, but don't focus on the negative. Do not let people speak into your life about your kids or to them if you're not convinced they love and care for them. I had to deal with this as well. I was foolishly tearing down Paul and my children because of what others said about them. Drop the 'tude, and you will start to see a change in your relationships. Begin to focus on the good. Many of us are married to good men, but we miss the forest for the trees. Refocus, and you'll rebuild your home. Ask God to help you renew your mind.

Building begins in our minds and is then acted out. I once heard a radio preacher say, "Our thoughts are a dress rehearsal for our actions." Let God's Word influence your thoughts toward your husband, and your attitude and actions will follow suit. Make it your goal to discover all the great things about your spouse. Meditate on these. Talk about them to your friends and family, and you'll see your 'tude begin to change. Sometimes you have to see things through eyes of faith. Stop treating your husband like a moron and begin to see him as a king, a great provider and lover. Call out the king in him and not the boy. You have the power to help that man become all God has called him to be. Yes, it can be hard to see anything good, but girl, you'd better faith it until full manifestation. Right now, the results you're getting are directly correlated to what you see of your man, which affects how you treat him or act toward him.

I heard one preacher say, "Where the focus goes, the power flows." Focus on the good things about your husband and power will flow there, producing the desired results. Now let me be real here: the day you begin to focus on the good is the day your husband might act crazy or do something to ride your righteous nerves. It's just a test you need to pass. Do not be discouraged. Be steadfast and immovable in your resolve to build your home.

> *And now, dear brothers and sisters, one final thing.*
> *Fix your thoughts on what is true, and honorable, and*
> *right, and pure, and lovely, and admirable. Think*
> *about things that are excellent and worthy of praise.*
> **Philippians 4:8 NLT**

DO YOU BUILD UP OR TEAR DOWN?

A foolish woman allows thoughts of her husband to be negative and allows others to influence her thoughts. A wise woman casts down every negative thought and chooses to allow the Word of God to influence her attitude.

DISCUSSION QUESTIONS

1. What is "the 'tude"?

2. When do you most struggle with your 'tude?

3. How does focusing on the negatives work like a magnifying glass?

4. Write down five things you admire about your husband and make it a practice to read them aloud each day for thirty days. Share with the group your observations about your attitude toward your husband.

CHAPTER 4

CAN I EXCHANGE MY GIFT?

And don't be wishing you were someplace else or with someone else. Where you are right now is God's place for you. Live and obey and love and believe right there. God, not your marital status, defines your life. Don't think I'm being harder on you than on the others. I give this same counsel in all the churches.
1 Corinthians 7:17 MSG

In early 2011, I was traveling to Zimbabwe and had a layover in Atlanta. I saw a billboard in one of the terminals with a picture of a polar bear and a fish inside an ice cube. The caption read:

"Opportunity does not always come perfectly gift-wrapped."

How true this rings for many things in our lives. Business opportunities don't always come perfectly wrapped; we have to work on them and do our due diligence.

Our mates are gifts from God, and they don't come perfectly gift-wrapped (and neither do we).

God gives us mates as an opportunity for growth and cultivation of the fruit of the Spirit. A foolish woman tears down her house by looking at the imperfectly wrapped package and asking for a gift exchange before she takes the time to open it.

Here in the States, gift exchanges are big right after Christmas. The lines for exchanges and returns are long because people aren't happy with their gift and want to exchange it for something else.

If you find yourself in line for a gift exchange because you don't think you got the right mate, I encourage you to exit that line, go home, unwrap your gift, and enjoy it. If you view your mate as the wrong person for you, you'll destroy your home. You will be fixated on the grass that looks greener on the other side and miss the perfect gift in imperfect wrapping right before your eyes. The 20 percent on the other side will begin to look better than the 80 percent you already have. It's a trick of the devil to make us think our gift is not good enough. The enemy is still using the same tricks on women as he did in the Garden of Eden.

> *The serpent was the shrewdest of all the wild animals the Lord God had made. One day he asked the woman, "Did God really say you must not eat the fruit from any of the trees in the garden?"*
>
> *"Of course we may eat fruit from the trees in the garden," the woman replied. "It's only the fruit from the tree in the middle of the garden that we are not allowed to eat. God said, 'You must not eat it or even touch it; if you do, you will die.'"*
>
> *"You won't die!" the serpent replied to the woman. "God knows that your eyes will be opened as soon as you eat it, and you will be like God, knowing both good and evil."*
> **Genesis 3:1–5 NLT**

The enemy succeeded in convincing Eve the 80 percent she had wasn't good enough, to instead go for the 20 percent, which ultimately resulted in her demise. The enemy is skillful in allowing us to think we could have done better, or maybe if we were not saved when we got together and now that we are saved, we should not still be with that person. The apostle Paul tells the church in 1 Corinthians 7:17 (NLT):

> *Each of you should continue to live in whatever situation the Lord has placed you, and remain as you were when God first called you. This is my rule for all the churches.*

I like the version in *The Message* as well:

> *And don't be wishing you were someplace else or with someone else. Where you are right now is God's place for you. Live and obey and love and believe right there. God, not your marital status, defines your life. Don't think I'm being harder on you than on the others. I give this same counsel in all the churches.*

The foolish woman thinks the grass is greener on the other side. She believes in her heart she made a mistake and could've done better. I spoke to a woman who said when she and her husband came together, they were "in the world," and she now questioned if her marriage was from the Lord. She felt she could have done better if she had married a man of God. Her husband had since become a man of God, but he still had faults, as do we all. I told her to cut out that kind of talk because she was going to talk herself out of a good marriage.

As women, it's always good to ask ourselves, *If my husband thought and acted toward me as though I wasn't right for him or he could have done better, how would I feel?* We often forget our husbands have feelings, too, and we mistake their silence as being happy and not seeing any faults in us. If my husband were to point out all the wrong things I do, all my imperfections, I'd be heartbroken and probably not recover. Yet we're doing the same to our husbands all the time, but they remain silent.

Maybe your mate is not the best; maybe he does not have the money to give you everything. Don't kid yourself into thinking you could have done better. Many foolish women have left their homes and kids in search of better only to find that what they had wasn't so bad after all. As I said, attitude is everything.

I'm not minimizing the fact that every marriage faces unmet expectations, which can influence our attitudes. We all go into marriage with certain expectations, both realistic and unrealistic, and when they aren't met, the result can be a negative attitude and a desire to leave the relationship. Always make sure you have the correct expectations of marriage. Your husband is not designed to meet all your needs and desires and to make you whole. Period. We all have a vacuum only God can fill.

Your husband is God's gift to you—he's imperfectly gift-wrapped but waiting to be enjoyed. Don't let years go by where you're standing in the exchange line, only to realize, after five, ten, fifteen, or even thirty-plus years, that your receipt says, "All sales final. No exchanges or returns."

If you read further on the receipt, you'll find this notice: "If there is a defect with your product, contact the manufacturer directly." Go to Jesus with your concerns, and He will show you how to enjoy your gift. He will remind you that you are to submit to your husband as unto Him. You are to love him through Christ. He will also remind you that man is imperfect and can disappoint you time and again, but He still desires we look to Him as our help in the time of uncertainty.

As my mother, Dr. Eunor Guti, wrote in her book *A Wise Woman*, "Your husband is your perfect shoe size."[2] Love him, respect him, and pray for him. Go and build; stop destroying him. Repent today. Your husband will suffer if you are angry all the time. He hasn't left, because he fears God. Let God change your attitude. God touched me and opened my eyes to the gift I had. Study him, and learn him all over again. There's more to him than what you see. Open your gift and enjoy it. Take time to tinker and play around with your gift, and you'll discover more about your husband. He is a better man than you think. He is God's gift to you!

DO YOU BUILD UP OR TEAR DOWN?
A foolish woman spends her time wishing for the 20 percent out of her reach while neglecting the 80 percent that is hers. A wise woman accepts her gift, studies it, and enjoys it.

DISCUSSION QUESTIONS

1. What is the danger in focusing on the 20 percent you don't have versus the 80 percent you do have?

2. Was your husband designed to meet all your needs? Who can?

3. What does it mean to you that "your husband is your perfect shoe size"?

CHAPTER 5

THE NAGGER

> *It is better to dwell in a corner of a housetop,*
> *Than in a house shared with a contentious woman.*
> **Proverbs 25:24 NKJV**

> *It's better to live alone in the corner of an attic*
> *than with a quarrelsome wife in a lovely home.*
> **Proverbs 25:24 NLT**

> *It's better to live alone in the desert*
> *than with a quarrelsome, complaining wife.*
> **Proverbs 21:19 NLT**

I find these Scriptures so powerful and quite funny. The poor man begins on the housetop and ends up in the desert, all to avoid his nagging wife. This is something the Lord continues to work out in me when interacting with my husband and children. Nagging our kids can result in reduced productivity and low self-esteem. (I know it first-hand. I'm still a work in progress.) Is your husband like the man who has to escape or work late because he knows the nagging will start as soon as he gets home? Of course, nowadays wives don't even have to wait until the husbands get home: there are cell phones! We can begin nagging as soon as we know they're driving home. We text-nag throughout the day. Instead of texting some sweet things, we nag through technology.

Scripture makes it clear that this poor man dreads being home. He'd rather stay late at work. He even volunteers to be the one who locks up, in the hope that when he gets home, his wife will be either too tired to nag or—even better—already asleep. The more he dreads coming home, the more a female coworker who celebrates him catches his attention, providing a tempting opportunity for an extramarital affair—maybe sexual, but usually emotional. Many saved men know it's a sin to commit adultery but can justify an emotional affair as having someone to "confide in."

Paul and I were part of a small group for couples, which consisted of his siblings, their spouses, and another couple. We met on Sunday nights to discuss our relationships. Openness and honesty were encouraged. Spouses could share what they wanted their spouse to work on, then give report next week. You didn't want to be the one whose report card said *Incomplete* or *Needs Improvement*! It was at these meetings that Paul revealed I was a nag. *Me? A nag? No!* At least, that's what I thought. As the saying goes, perception is reality. I didn't think I was a nag, but my husband sure thought so.

It was then we came up with a policy in our home: If something needed doing, we agreed on a deadline. I was not to remind him of the task at hand during this time, even if I saw opportunities for completion. If the responsible party (usually Paul) didn't ask for an extension, post-deadline it was fair game to bring it up and remind him (or nag, for lack of a better term). He was motivated to keep me quiet, so he often got the task done ahead of time or requested an extension. This just about cured nagging in our house, though the "nag monster" slips out now and then.

I write this feeling a little convicted because Paul often asks me to take care of something—maybe replace a missing button, check on someone, send a thank-you card—but if I don't complete my task in the allotted time, he's patient and tries not to browbeat me. Whereas I am quick to get on him for not following through, "as usual."

Think about your home. If your husband doesn't (for the most part) nag you when you fail to complete your task, then why should you nag him? Jesus admonishes us to remove the huge log in our own eye before removing the tiny splinter in another person's eye.

In Judges 16, Delilah nagged Samson until he divulged the secret to his strength. Now *that* is some serious nagging—and the fast track to destroying a home. If a woman nags her husband long enough, eventually, just to get some sanity and peace, he will give in to whatever she wants, even if it will bring harm to the family. My husband preached on this nagging woman one day and raised an interesting point. I'd always wondered why Samson would give in to Delilah while knowing what she was about. Every time he told her where his strength came from, she tested it. I would think after the first time she tied him up with ropes and called in the Philistines, he'd have realized this lady was up to no good. But the power of nagging eventually brought Samson down. He knew she was working for the Philistines, but the power of the nagger drove him to reveal his secret.

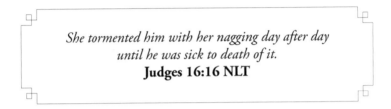

She tormented him with her nagging day after day until he was sick to death of it.
Judges 16:16 NLT

Sometimes, as a foolish woman, I nag about the things Paul is not getting done, but if I ask myself if I've finished everything he asked *me* to do, the answer is a resounding "No!" As I write, I'm reminded of a button he asked me to replace on his white shirt. It's been a few years now, but he's never once nagged me about it. Shame on me!

It's easy to mistake our husbands' silence for happiness or contentment. Don't fall into that trap and find yourself in a struggling marriage because you assumed your husband was happy just because he didn't nag as you do.

DO YOU BUILD UP OR TEAR DOWN?

A foolish woman drives her husband away by constant nagging and badgering. A wise woman negotiates with her husband and assumes the best of him.

DISCUSSION QUESTIONS

1. What does Scripture say about a nagging, quarrelsome wife?

2. What is one danger to a marriage that can be caused by a nagging wife?

3. The author describes a creative policy she and her husband utilize to reduce nagging. What policy could you and your husband put in place to increase the peace in your marriage?

CHAPTER 6

THE GRUDGE-HOLDER

If you forgive those who sin against you, your heavenly Father will forgive you. But if you refuse to forgive others, your Father will not forgive your sins.
Matthew 6:14–15 NLT

Sometime earlier in our marriage, my husband wronged me and hurt my feelings. We exchanged words, but because I didn't know how to express my hurt and disappointment, I kept quiet and held the wrong against him. Each morning I went into my closet to pray and cry out to God, but I couldn't break through in prayer. I would speak to Paul only when he spoke to me because we had agreed to never give each other the silent treatment.

Let me pause here and encourage those waiting to be married to ensure you and your mate decide from the start what kind of marriage you're going to have and how you will relate to one another. Some things Paul and I agreed upon were not to use silent treatment; never to yell at one another; not to slam doors, no matter how angry we get; not to drive off in anger; and, of course, not to let the sun go down on our wrath. Have we been perfect? No! But we do have a standard we strive to live by.

Back to my story, I spoke tersely to my husband because I was fooling myself into thinking I wasn't breaking our code of conduct. I felt justified in holding his sin toward me in my heart. I wanted him to come to me and apologize again because I didn't feel he was sincere when he had apologized. Thank God for the Holy Spirit who convicts us of sin!

> *And when he comes, he will convict the world of its*
> *sin, and of God's righteousness, and of the coming*
> *judgment.*
> **John 16:8 NLT**

I remember one morning as I was praying, I felt like Jacob when he wrestled with God. The Holy Spirit was reminding me that I was wrong to hold the offense against my husband while still expecting God to forgive me. God's Word is clear on this matter:

> *If you forgive those who sin against you, your heavenly*
> *Father will forgive you. But if you refuse to forgive*
> *others, your Father will not forgive your sins.*
> **Matthew 6:14–15 NLT**

God knows and understands when we are wronged, but somehow I was reading the Bible as saying that I could hold on to my unforgiveness until my husband apologized properly to me.

It's a foolish woman who thinks God understands and grants her exception to His Word. I was that foolish woman, praying each morning and expecting God to forgive me while I wouldn't forgive my husband. That morning when I wrestled with the Holy Spirit, I pleaded my case to Him, but He did not budge. I was to go to Paul, start talking, and ask him for forgiveness. Let me tell you, I fought and flat out told God no! But He kept tugging at my heart until I surrendered, because ultimately my desire is to please Him. A Scripture that has since become real to me is this simple verse:

> *Blessed are the pure in heart, for they shall see God.*
> **Matthew 5:8 NKJV**

I desire to see Him, so I need to keep my heart pure and free from unforgiveness. I had to die to my flesh, even though I felt justified, and walk in the Spirit so I would not fulfill the lusts of the flesh.

So I say, let the Holy Spirit guide your lives. Then you won't be doing what your sinful nature craves. The sinful nature wants to do evil, which is just the opposite of what the Spirit wants. And the Spirit gives us desires that are the opposite of what the sinful nature desires. These two forces are constantly fighting each other, so you are not free to carry out your good intentions.…

When you follow the desires of your sinful nature, the results are very clear: sexual immorality, impurity, lustful pleasures, idolatry, sorcery, hostility, quarreling, jealousy, outbursts of anger, selfish ambition, dissension, division, envy, drunkenness, wild parties, and other sins like these. Let me tell you again, as I have before, that anyone living that sort of life will not inherit the Kingdom of God.

But the Holy Spirit produces this kind of fruit in our lives: love, joy, peace, patience, kindness, goodness, faithfulness, gentleness, and self-control. There is no law against these things!

Those who belong to Christ Jesus have nailed the passions and desires of their sinful nature to his cross and crucified them there. Since we are living by the Spirit, let us follow the Spirit's leading in every part of our lives.
Galatians 5:16–17, 19–25 NLT

Sometimes we hold our husbands to a higher standard than we do ourselves. We act as though they had better not wrong us because we won't let them forget it. But when *we* err and wrong our husbands, we want them to forgive quickly and be Christlike by not treating us according to our iniquities. When we hold grudges or refuse to forgive, we let a cancer spread in our relationships.

Even if you have been wronged repeatedly, you need to forgive. Yes, there are times when a wrong that is committed takes time for healing to take place, but forgiveness still has to take place. I once heard a lady say, "Forgiveness is such a hard word." She's absolutely right: forgiveness *is* hard. But God still commands us to do so if we want Him to forgive us.

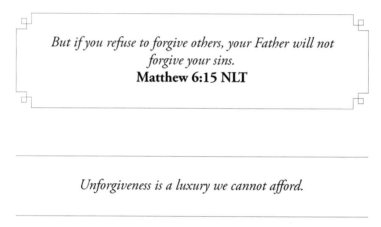

> But if you refuse to forgive others, your Father will not forgive your sins.
> **Matthew 6:15 NLT**

Unforgiveness is a luxury we cannot afford.

Unforgiveness in any relationship, especially in marriage, is a cancer that will destroy not only the relationship but you, your husband, and your children. Some of us have been praying and fasting, but due to our harboring unforgiveness, God is not hearing. Our prayers sound like noise to Him.

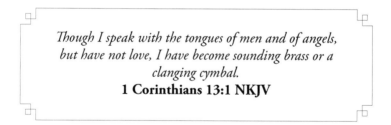

> Though I speak with the tongues of men and of angels, but have not love, I have become sounding brass or a clanging cymbal.
> **1 Corinthians 13:1 NKJV**

I picture God wearing earplugs. He can see our mouths moving, but He can't hear us. We have to forgive today and make our relationship right with both God and our husbands. You have to forgive for healing to come into your home.

DO YOU BUILD UP OR TEAR DOWN?

*A foolish woman has an unforgiving heart and refuses to obey
the Word of God. A wise woman is quick to forgive, though it
may be difficult, knowing that for her sins to be forgiven, she
must forgive.*

DISCUSSION QUESTIONS

1. Does God's understanding extend to unforgiveness? Why or why not?

2. What happens when we refuse to forgive?

3. Where is God calling you to offer forgiveness to your spouse today?

CHAPTER 7

MINEFIELD

> *Who can find a virtuous and capable wife? She is more*
> *precious than rubies. Her husband can trust her, and*
> *she will greatly enrich his life. She brings him good,*
> *not harm, all the days of her life.*
> **Proverbs 31:10–12 NLT**

I n 1996, Graça Machel, then-wife of former Mozambican president Samora Machel, published a report for UNICEF, "The Impact of Armed Conflict on Children." Another topic she addressed, "Land-mines: A Deadly Inheritance," was of particular interest. A landmine is a bomb buried in the ground that explodes when one steps on or drives over it. Machel detailed the damage they had caused communities, especially the danger they posed to children. Her report stated:

Over 110 million land-mines of various types—plus millions more unexploded bombs, shells, and grenades—remain hidden around the world, waiting to be triggered by the innocent and unsuspecting. The victims of the landmine explosion are usually killed or at least maimed.[3]

A foolish woman's house is like a minefield, where the husband
is afraid to speak up or do anything for fear of triggering a
landmine.

In order to avoid landmines, he has to tiptoe through the home and pray to God he doesn't set one off. A foolish woman's husband has to tread lightly in his own house because it is not a safe place but a war zone, a minefield. At any given moment a landmine can explode if he does something wrong, or doesn't correctly handle how money is being spent, and so on. Some men have been reduced to nothing and can't take control of their house because of the landmines foolish women have set. Some men have no say in what happens with the money or in raising the children. In order to avoid explosions, they withdraw and begin to slowly die from the inside.

A foolish woman destroys her home by not creating a safe haven where her husband can express his feelings, hurts, disappointments, and struggles without being ridiculed or looked down on. As a wife, you should strive to be a woman whose heart your husband can safely trust in, like the Proverbs 31 lady:

> *Who can find a virtuous and capable wife? She is more*
> *precious than rubies. Her husband can trust her, and*
> *she will greatly enrich his life. She brings him good,*
> *not harm, all the days of her life.*
> **Proverbs 31:10–12 NLT**

This wise woman created a safe haven for her husband to pour out his heart. She didn't use it against him or belittle him. We have to work to win our husbands' trust because every man needs a listening ear, not judging lips.

If we don't create safe havens for our husbands, we may drive them into the arms of other women who will listen and not judge them. If your husband never shares any intimate issues with you about what's on his heart or mind, then you haven't created a safe haven for him. You might think he's supposed to be strong and confident all the time and know exactly what to do, but that is not so. We can be so preoccupied talking through our issues (even though that's the way God designed us to be) that we forget that our husbands have needs, too. They are often unsure what to do and shoulder the burden of leading and providing for the family. Most men are dealing with a lot of pressure on the job and need an escape. We must be like the woman in Song of Solomon who drew her man in and allowed him to be himself without passing judgment.

"The look," which I'll talk more about later, is usually the way we pass judgment if we have a little more sense than to belittle our husbands verbally. The women without even that much sense tell their husbands to man up, take leadership, and stop whining. That does not create a safe haven but a nest of thistles that could tempt your husband to seek a safe haven elsewhere.

Not long ago, Paul and I were driving through downtown Chicago and talking. He told me there were some things he'd love to share with me; he said he trusted me but was afraid of the look I might give him while he poured out his heart. It broke my heart to know he felt this way. I realized I still have work to do. We have a healthy marriage, which we are constantly working on, and that day, I learned a new area where I still need to work to prevent the enemy from gaining a foothold.

Notice in Proverbs the strange woman Solomon speaks of who knows how to create the *illusion* of a safe haven:

> *She threw her arms around him and kissed him, and with a brazen look she said, "I've just made my peace offerings and fulfilled my vows. You're the one I was looking for! I came out to find you, and here you are! My bed is spread with beautiful blankets, with colored sheets of Egyptian linen. I've perfumed my bed with myrrh, aloes, and cinnamon. Come, let's drink our fill of love until morning. Let's enjoy each other's caresses, for my husband is not home. He's away on a long trip. He has taken a wallet full of money with him and won't return until later this month." So she seduced him with her pretty speech and enticed him with her flattery.*
> **Proverbs 7:13–21 NLT**

She is skillful in her enticement by providing a safe haven for him. She reassures him everything is okay; things will work out. As women, we need to hear this from our husbands as well: things will work out; we'll pull through the financial mess; we'll raise our children to fear God and they will turn out all right; things will work out at the job where a co-worker seems determined to cause problems. Just as we need a safe haven, our husbands need one even more.

We must verbalize our trust, even if we don't see clearly the direction he leads. We have to realize he's under a lot of pressure to perform on the job, even if things are tough on us at home. We need to stop demanding things when we know our finances are tight and the family lives on a budget.

I know all too well that what I'm saying is not easy, especially when there are needs at home. We may be frustrated and want answers now, but we must first create a safe haven to keep him engaged and connected. If we do this well, we will receive the answers we need and the emotional connection we crave.

A constantly unhappy wife creates an unsafe haven. No man wants to come home to a wife who is always sad and communicates her unhappiness with the life she has with him. A godly man desires to please his wife and make her happy, but if he feels like she will never be happy no matter how hard he tries, he will simply give up and try to avoid her.

A contributing factor to an unsafe haven is a messy home. A wife could think that just because her husband is not as neat as she is, he doesn't want a clean house. A man may be tempted to stay away from his house because it's dirty and disorganized.

I enjoy home-decorating and reorganizing shows. In one episode, the wife was a hoarder and the husband just wanted to be able to walk from room to room without feeling like he was going through an obstacle course. Adding to the chaos, they had children and pets. I was surprised the husband hadn't been driven away by the mess. One issue that came out in the discussion was their sex life was suffering. The wife stayed home all day but never found time to clean herself, the kids, or the house. When the husband came back from work, he had to clean up the children, then help get food—cooked on a dirty stove—on the table. It was both gross and sad to watch.

Let's learn from the wise woman in Proverbs 31 who knows how to create that space where her husband can be himself and doesn't have to walk in fear of setting off a landmine. Our homes should be places of escape, peace, and safety.

DO YOU BUILD UP OR TEAR DOWN?

A foolish woman makes her home an unsafe place of contention and stress. A wise woman creates a safe place where her husband can be vulnerable and secure.

DISCUSSION QUESTIONS

1. Compare and contrast what a home looks like as a minefield versus a safe haven.

2. What can happen if a husband does not find his home to be a safe haven?

3. How does the cleanliness and organization of your home affect your spouse?

CHAPTER 8

"THE LOOK"

How we handle our husbands' shortcomings reveals more about our own character than our husbands'.
— **Courtney Joseph**

G rowing up, my mom would give us a look if we were behaving inappropriately, especially if we had company or if she wanted us to do something without making a public announcement. We kids all knew what the look meant; it spoke volumes, and we knew to straighten up, or else. Even now she can still communicate that way with us. Only now, amongst other things, that look is to show her disapproval of how we are treating or communicating with our husbands. Her look still elicits the same results. We have to straighten up or else we'll face Mom and Dad's wrath behind closed doors. Their parenting has not stopped just because we are married with children, and I thank God for that.

A wife can give that same momma-look to her husband. But in marriage, the message that the look communicates is different.

A wife doesn't have to say anything but can communicate volumes through her look of disdain, disapproval, dislike, and disgust.

This is also called the look of contempt. John Gottman writes, "Contempt is fueled by long-simmering negative thoughts about the partner. You're more likely to think such thoughts if your differences are not resolved."[4] He states when contempt is present in a marriage, it's headed for divorce unless there is immediate intervention. As a wife, if you neglect to address issues or concerns you have with your husband, your feelings will come out through your body language. Those feelings will slip out no matter how hard you try to bottle them in.

The look not only communicates disgust, but it also implies impending consequences, such as withholding intimacy, a rundown of all the negative things about him, silent treatment, etc. I am guilty of using the look, and many times my husband has called me on it because it spoke volumes to him. With one look I communicated to him that he, at that moment, was not good for anything, that I could not depend on him, and that he was less of a man and not worthy of my respect.

Instead of answering back, I began to use the look like a weapon of negative communication. *Better than talking back,* I figured, but I was actually still saying volumes with the look. I thought I was taking the moral high ground by not speaking anything negative. I seemed to be the submissive and agreeable wife, but I was struggling with unresolved issues. I wasn't handling my husband's shortcomings in a healthy way, and that spoke volumes about *me*. I progressed in my skillful use of the look until Psalm 119:130 began to shed light on this bad habit:

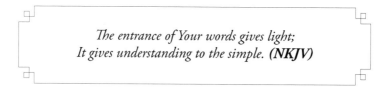

The entrance of Your words gives light;
It gives understanding to the simple. (NKJV)

My dear sister, do not fool yourself into thinking you are being a good wife or extra-spiritual by holding your tongue while using the look to talk back. The look can also be manifested through rolling eyes, sighs, throwing up arms, stern stares, etc. All of these nonverbal demonstrations can break down a man, push him away, and even lead to destruction in a marriage.

It is important to understand that contempt arises when a wife feels unheard and her attempts to be heard and understood have failed. This, of course, is not a healthy way of communicating issues. Sometimes our concerns are unheard and misunderstood because of the way we present them. How the message is delivered is just as important, if not more important, than the message itself. As wives, we often shoot ourselves in the foot by allowing our emotions to get the better of us when communicating with our husbands. Remember men are usually logical thinkers and appreciate clear messages. If you are feeling super emotional, take a time-out to gather yourself and then communicate clearly. Crying and emotional outbursts can create noise in your communication that dominates and muffles the message you are trying to communicate.

Learn to complain without criticizing or showing contempt.

1. A *complaint* is specific—e.g., "I'm upset because you did not put your dishes away."

2. *Criticism* uses sweeping statements (often with words like *always* and *never*) and blames—e.g., "You never put the dishes away; I always have to do it."

3. *Contempt* adds character assassination and insults to the criticism—e.g., "You never put the dishes away; I always have to do it. You're just lazy!"

   - Try using the A-B-C Principle. [A] is the action that prompted your complaint; [B] is the context/situation in which it occurred; [C] is how you felt. It takes this approximate format: *"When you did [A] in the [B] (situation), I felt [C]."* Here's a practical example: "When you joked about my cooking when we had guests over earlier, I felt mocked." You can also try using the Sandwich Principle where you sandwich a complaint or criticism between two compliments.

   - Another variation of the A-B-C Principle is to state the **action**, how you **feel**, and what you would like **changed** or what you **need**. For example: "When you speak harshly to me, I feel belittled and uncared for and find myself becoming defensive. I would like for you to speak kindly to me because I know you don't mean to hurt me."

4. Watch your tone—don't be intimidating or belligerent by saying things like: "What's your complaint? Speak up!" or "What is it this time? Here we go again!"

DO YOU BUILD UP OR TEAR DOWN?
A foolish woman uses "the Look" to communicate disagreement to her husband. A wise woman deals with unresolved issues to avoid breeding contempt in her marriage.

DISCUSSION QUESTIONS

1. What is "the look"?

2. How can the look affect communication between marriage partners?

3. What would be a better option instead of using the look?

CHAPTER 9

CONCEALED WEAPON

The words of the reckless pierce like swords,
but the tongue of the wise brings healing.
Proverbs 12:18 NIV

P roverbs 12 describes the words of the reckless as a piercing sword that leaves trails of blood everywhere. The tongue is like a concealed weapon: it can seem harmless, and sometimes you don't even see it, but it can damage people, destroy relationships, and attack the very essence of personhood. James 3:6–7 calls the tongue "a fire, a world of wickedness." This small tongue is restless, evil, and full of deadly poison if not tamed or submitted to the law of kindness or Word of God. God created woman unique from man, and one main difference is found in our speech. Scientists have concluded that women use about twice as many words as men! That in itself is not the problem; it's *how* we use those words. Most men are not very talkative and rarely win debates with their wives. A wife can outtalk him both in *number* of words and in how she *articulates* them. A foolish woman misuses her words and causes bleeding in her home.

A foolish woman can insult and cut her husband down with
just a few words or a look.

There have been many times I spoke cutting words to my husband because I did not approve of something he did or he didn't do what I wanted him to. When I saw my words hurt not only his feelings but his ego and manhood, I had to repent.

"From the fruit of their lips people enjoy good things" (Proverbs 13:2a NIV). But lips can produce good or bad fruit. The choice is yours.

Whatever you're experiencing in your marriage is a result of the words you've spoken. Whatever you are seeing in your husband is a result of the words you have spoken to him or about him. A foolish woman knows how to destroy her husband with her words. Many women complain their husbands aren't engaged at home, don't participate, don't lead, etc. When I hear this, I'm led to ask: "How do you talk to your husband? Do you build him up, or are your words condescending and insulting?" Maybe his lack of leadership is caused by a sharp tongue that constantly cuts him down. We often hear hurtful, mean remarks immediately followed by "I'm just saying." People use this phrase as if it magically renders anything they say harmless and inoffensive.

Determine today to use your abundance of words to bring life, not death; to heal relationships, not wound them. Reserve your bank of words for your time in prayer. Our words have power, and because of the influence God has given us, they're that much more powerful to build or tear down.

> *Wives, likewise, be submissive to your own husbands, that even if some do not obey the word, they, without a word, may be won by the conduct of their wives, when they observe your chaste conduct accompanied by fear.*
> **1 Peter 3:1–2 NKJV**

I heard a woman share one time that when she began to put this into practice, her home changed, and now her husband is saved and serving the Lord. The foolish woman can be a stumbling block to her husband's committing to Christ because if this Jesus she serves makes her behave like this, then he doesn't want any part of Him. The foolish woman gives her local church a bad name because after years of attending church, there is no change in her.

I was once faced with a problem at the church from a woman who attended every women's meeting and prayer time but acted like a devil at home. Her husband told me he didn't think I was teaching the Word at the meetings because he didn't see any change in his wife. Her behavior was confusing to him because the tongue she used to lead worship and bless the Lord was the same tongue she used to curse her husband. I confronted her: if she wasn't open to change, she would be unwelcome at meetings because she was discrediting God's work with her foolish behavior and sharp tongue. Dear friend, you're not fooling anyone when you're ever-so-sweet to your pals and your pastor, but at home are the devil incarnate, piercing and wounding people with your sword-like tongue.

As I was writing this chapter, sitting in the Atlanta airport and waiting for our connecting flight, I had the opportunity to practice what I was preaching. We had a two-hour layover, and my oldest daughter had the bright idea of purchasing Pop-Tarts with her money. (She knew there was no way I'd use my hard-earned money to buy something like that.) She, of course, shared the Pop-Tarts with her brother and sister. After Paul returned from hunting down some decent coffee, our kids asked if he could take them on the Plane Train, the train that connects the different terminals.

Being the wonderful dad he is, he consented. So I watched him walk away with three sugar-high kids. They rode the train to different terminals, but when they returned to Terminal C, the children decided to run ahead of their father. Watching them speed off, Paul waited, knowing they would turn around to see if he was behind. He waited five minutes, then ten, but no sign of our children in the world's busiest airport.

As the boarding time drew near, I called Paul to find out how close they were to returning to our gate. He told me he might have lost the children but was waiting for them to come back. About five minutes later he called me and simply said, "The kids are officially lost. Get down here and help me look for them!" We then decided I should stay put because the children knew the gate number and might show up there—or at least this was our hope. We prayed together and then we waited.

Allow me to let you into my mind for a moment. Before, I would have panicked, asked Paul how he could have lost the children, and pointed out he was responsible for this. My emotions would have been on full-blast, and swords would have been flying out of my mouth. Yet *I remained calm!* This was rather unusual for me.

A couple of minutes after we prayed, the children showed up. I called Paul to tell him the kids were back as he was about to engage a TSA agent. Stern words were spoken, biblical correction was promised, and the drama was over. I thanked God that our children were seated a few rows behind us, because their father was enraged.

A special blessing for me in all this was the fact that Paul noticed the lack of verbal swords flying in his direction. God had enabled me to remain calm in a very stressful situation.

A foolish woman destroys her home with her sharp tongue, but a wise woman builds her house by giving a soft answer and displaying Christlike conduct. Her speech is governed by the Word of God and the law of kindness. When she opens her mouth, her husband does not have to take cover because arrows are going to fly out.

> *She opens her mouth with wisdom,*
> *And on her tongue is the law of kindness.*
> **Proverbs 31:26 NKJV**

In their book *Every Woman's Marriage*, Shannon and Greg Ethridge[5] share some helpful ways of communicating that can prevent us from tearing down our homes. I have also included a few of my own examples below:

Words of Judgment: "Well, it's about time you called. I hate it when I don't hear from you all day."

Words of Encouragement: "You must be really busy today, but I'm so glad you found a moment to call. I miss your voice."

Words of Judgment: "If I know you, you're probably not going to follow through on this project, so why bother?"

Words of Encouragement: "I know this isn't really your cup of tea, so I'm proud of you for trying to tackle this yourself."

Words of Judgment: "That's just like you, always doing stuff for others and putting our family last."

Words of Encouragement: "I think it's wonderful you want to help this person. Before you make a commitment, though, can we talk about what effect this might have on our time together as a family?"

Words of Judgment: "All you ever want is to have sex. Don't you see I'm tired? You just sit around and wait in bed for me without helping me."

Words of Encouragement: "I really appreciate your desire for me. I don't have to worry about whether or not you're into me. It makes me feel good as your wife. Sometimes I'm really tired and may need you to help me get in the mood or even help put the children to bed or clean up the kitchen while I take a shower and prepare for you. My desire is to fully engage with you."

Words of Judgment: "You really smell and need to take a shower before you come to bed or try to touch me."

Words of Encouragement: "Wow, you've had a really long day. Working hard lifting those boxes must have been tiring, not to mention making you sweaty. A good shower always helps relax and refresh you. Let's take one together. Or while you take a shower, I will prepare for you."

Words of Judgment: "Why don't you hold my hand in public like other couples do? Are you ashamed of me or are you not man enough to show affection?"

Words of Encouragement: *[reach for his hand]* "I feel so special and loved when you hold my hand. It fills up my love tank. I know it's a small thing, but it does wonders for me."

Words of Judgment: "You've been stuck at your dead-end job. Don't you have any ambition in life, or do I have to have ambition for the both of us?"

Words of Encouragement: "Your job is lucky to have a hard worker like you. You rarely take time off and are very productive. Your skills have grown, and I was just thinking that because you're a hard worker—and sadly, not everyone always is—you might start looking into other positions that will increase your skills and make you an even bigger asset to the company. You're a quick learner and I have no doubt you'd excel in a new position."

DO YOU BUILD UP OR TEAR DOWN?
A foolish woman destroys her home with her sharp tongue.
A wise woman builds her house by giving a soft answer and through her Christlike conduct.
A foolish woman's tongue is a sword that cuts down her husband (and others). A wise woman uses her tongue to build up her husband.

DISCUSSION QUESTIONS

1. How can your tongue be used as a weapon?

2. Instead of using her words for judgment, how does a wise woman use her words?

3. Write down two words of encouragement to use with your husband today.

4. Read James 3:1–12. Make notes on the areas the Holy Spirit highlights as areas of growth for you.

CHAPTER 10

I CAN DO IT BETTER

If a man's wife believes in him, he can conquer the world—or at least his little corner of it.
— **Shaunti Feldhahn**

Right before I was married, my future mother-in-law gave me some advice: Don't do the things your husband is supposed to do. Celebrate what he does, and don't criticize him when he tries to help. She added that I should go so far as to act like I don't know how to do anything he is supposed to do. I didn't understand it at first, but I took her advice to heart.

Every Monday, which was our day off, Paul and I cleaned the house. He took on the vacuuming, and I celebrated and praised his vacuuming abilities to the point even now he always vacuums if our kids aren't around. I tell him he does a better job than I do. When we had our first child, Lydia, I remember Paul changing her diapers. With girls, there are a few more areas to clean, and at times he didn't get all of it 100 percent clean, but I never told him he couldn't do a good job. I sometimes just waited for an opportune time to fix it without telling him I could do a better job than he.

The foolish woman takes every opportunity she can to talk about how she makes better decisions. Whenever her husband tries to lead and make decisions, the foolish woman undermines him and makes him feel incapable of doing anything right. To wives who do this, I want to ask: "Do you think he was capable of making a good decision when it came to marrying you? Then give him some credit!"

The foolish woman who acts like she's the only wise adult in the relationship may feel she can better handle the money, raise the kids, plan for the future, etc. But what usually happens is she becomes bitter because she feels she carries the burden for the family and has to do everything. It is important to remember that most men will not fight for position.

Another applicable area is in money matters. The percentage of women earning more than their husbands increased from 4 percent in 1970 to 22 percent in 2007.[6] The wise woman in Proverbs 31 is an example to women who earn more than their husbands. She is a businesswoman but doesn't take over. She uses her earning power to gain her husband more respect at home and the city gates. She doesn't hold her higher income against her husband and never makes him feel less of a provider. She understands she has a role to play in increasing the family's estate and does not spend it and complain when the money runs out.

If you've staged a coup in your household, begin today to relinquish the authority that is not yours. Yes, there are instances where the woman must lead because the man will not. If you are in that position, do what you need to do to keep your family functioning, but find ways to encourage him to claim his position. Point out things he does better than you and let him know you need his help. Take my mother-in-law's advice and act like you don't know how to do certain things in an effort to engage him. This will boost his ego and cause him to take his rightful position. One may call this manipulation, but a wise woman knows she has to do certain things to encourage her husband to lead. Consult him on major household decisions; don't make decisions and tell him later what you did. Only the foolish woman who wants to tear down her house will do this.

Make a determination today to get out of the driver's seat, because only one person can drive at a time. Allow him to drive. Allow him to take his God-given position. I understand that even though my husband is in the driver's seat, I can help navigate so that we are working together to arrive at the desired destination. It's not that your husband is more intelligent than you, but he has been assigned by God to lead you.

DO YOU BUILD UP OR TEAR DOWN?

A foolish woman holds on to the steering wheel because she doesn't trust her husband to lead. A wise woman prays for her husband and trusts God to lead him even if he is not saved.

DISCUSSION QUESTIONS

1. Why should you avoid doing the things your husband is supposed to do?

2. What are the dangers of manipulation in a marriage?

3. How does a woman who earns more money than her husband need to be sensitive to his headship?

CHAPTER 11

THE MOTHER SYNDROME

A worthy wife is a crown for her husband,
but a disgraceful woman is like cancer in his bones.
Proverbs 12:4 NLT

My husband and I had dinner with a couple, and by the time we parted that evening, I was mortified. During our discussions, the wife kept talking about how bad the husband was at handling money and taking care of business. Unfortunately, I also have my own story on this. My heart weeps every time I tell this story because as I said, when the foolish woman belittles her husband, she is usually unaware.

One summer I was privileged to have three of my sisters at one time in our home. One Friday we had to drop my husband at the barbershop before we went to the beauty supply store. As Paul was getting out of the car, I asked if he had his phone and his Bible, as he had mentioned he wanted to read and study at the barber. After he got out of the car, my sisters looked at me and asked why I talked to my husband like a child. I had not been aware of how I had been communicating with him. I know Paul doesn't like to forget things, and he's hard on himself when he does. I was simply trying to avoid him being disappointed, but in my effort to help, I came across as mothering.

Dr. Kevin Leman wrote a book on birth order and how it affects our relationships, especially in marriage and parenting.[7] Certain birth-order marriages are compatible and others spell struggles, though a couple can work through the issues. Acknowledging and understanding them is half the battle. Paul is the baby of his family, and I'm in the middle of mine, close to the top. I'm used to taking charge and getting things done, while he's used to things being done for him. I have to exercise sound judgment to allow him to take charge and be in control. Take time to discuss this with your husband, and you both might be enlightened.

My mother often tells of how her upbringing affected the way she dealt with men. She was raised with her brothers and *as* one of the brothers. When it came time to marry, she didn't know how to handle herself as a lady or even speak like one. She was used to being rough to keep up with her brothers. In fact, her dad didn't make much distinction between her and her brothers. Whatever they did, she did too. My father had to lovingly cultivate her, cleanse away the hardness with love and the Word, as Scripture says in Ephesians 5:25–28 (KJV)…

> *Husbands, love your wives, even as Christ also loved the church, and gave himself for it; that he might sanctify and cleanse it with the washing of water by the word, that he might present it to himself a glorious church, not having spot, or wrinkle, or any such thing; but that it should be holy and without blemish. So ought men to love their wives as their own bodies. He that loveth his wife loveth himself.*

Now my mother is the sweetest lady, submissive yet powerful.

The foolish woman belittles her husband in private and in public.

I've realized something about the foolish woman: she usually doesn't set off to belittle her husband, but no one ever taught her differently. Of course, other women knowingly belittle their husbands. Some women have been raised to think men are ignorant and cannot be trusted to do anything. In fact, through TV, society reinforces the stereotypically false "men are simple and clueless" notion. Take, for example, *The Cosby Show*, a popular sitcom now in syndication.

The Huxtables are a picture-perfect family. Both parents have successful careers. But have you noticed Clair Huxtable is always the sensible one who takes charge and makes good decisions, while Cliff is a good father but incapable of making good decisions? The kids would rather talk to their mom because Daddy is silly and doesn't understand. Some women have grown up with this picture and treat their husbands as complete idiots. If you're a foolish woman, this is one quick way to destroy your house.

Many men will not say anything or even appear to be bothered by this, but if another woman comes on the scene who treats him like a king, he may be tempted to gravitate toward her. The following is an excerpt from the book *Every Woman's Marriage*:

"I like it when my wife does nice things for me, such as packing my lunch or pressing my shirt the day before a big meeting, but sometimes she talks to me as if I'm not capable of doing things myself or making decisions on my own. Sometimes she tells me to bundle up, or else I'll catch cold (as if I can't tell how much outerwear I need a day), or she'll rudely insist that I change clothes because I'm not dressed appropriately for the occasion when what I am wearing is perfectly fine. I resent being told what to do. I am a man, and I have a pretty sharp mind of my own. I don't need or want someone telling me how to dress. It's humiliating."

Another man also expressed his frustrations in the same book:

"Whenever I'm out with my wife at social gatherings, she is always answering questions directed to me. It really gets to me when I'm with my friends who already think that my wife wears the pants. I feel like a child who needs mommy to answer questions above my head. I wish she knew what she is doing. She is destroying my manhood."[8]

This is sad, but the reality is, this is happening. I wish I could say I haven't committed the same trespasses. Thank God for His grace and mercy!

> *For the word of God is living and powerful, and sharper than any two-edged sword, piercing even to the division of soul and spirit, and of joints and marrow, and is a discerner of the thoughts and intents of the heart. And there is no creature hidden from His sight, but all things are naked and open to the eyes of Him to whom we must give account.*
> **Hebrews 4:12–13 NKJV**

Let's allow the Word to work in us because we have to give an account for the way we treated our husbands.

DO YOU BUILD UP OR TEAR DOWN?
A foolish woman treats her husband as her child. A wise woman honors her husband and reveres him as her head.

DISCUSSION QUESTIONS

1. How can our upbringing affect our approach to our marriage relationship?

2. Are you a wife who belittles her husband, either knowingly or unknowingly? Explain.

3. Have a conversation with your husband, asking him how he perceives your communication with him in private and in public.

CHAPTER 12

I'M NOT INTO WHAT HE'S INTO

The best marriages are blending of two people. While each person maintains his and her unique personality and interests, they both deliberately integrate those interests. When it's done right, each person becomes a happier and better person.
— **Willard F. Harley, Jr.**

I'm just not into what he's into. How many times have you heard that statement? I learned early in my marriage the importance of learning to like the things my husband likes so I don't drive him away or cause him to run to other people. My father always told me that my husband should find almost everything he needs in me, and that includes companionship.

In *Love and Respect*, Dr. Emerson Eggerichs writes about a man's need for companionship:

The wife who wants to show her husband that she likes him—that she is his friend—will be patient with his strange request to "just come out here and be with me. Watch what I am doing, or just watch TV with me, but let's not talk." When the husband calls the wife in to "just sit by him," he is working on their relationship in a significant way—not significant to her, perhaps, but extremely significant, nonetheless. This is the way a husband communicates. Males prefer shoulder-to-shoulder communication instead of face-to-face communication, and this can occur in the simplest of ways.[9]

This need for companionship can (and should) be primarily met by his wife, then by his guy friends. As a woman, if you always send your husband off because you are "not into what he's into," you might lose him to another woman who shows interest in what interests him.

Men have affairs with women who are not necessarily better-looking, but who know how to do what the wife is not doing at home.

This lady, whom the Bible calls the "strange woman" (Proverbs 7), speaks to her lover with great respect, does things in bed the wife is too shy or doesn't want to do, and is into the things he likes. The strange woman studies this man, knows where the gaps are, and seeks to fill them, while the wife sits at home, refusing to engage. Certain acts are not within the bounds of God's blessing and should never be permitted in the marriage bed. There are ways to deal with this matter in marriage, but it goes beyond the scope of this book. Seek godly counsel if you are struggling in this area.

As mentioned earlier, I had to learn to enjoy the things my husband enjoys. Paul loves basketball, but I didn't find it exciting. I'd rather watch a chick flick than basketball. When he would try to tell me all about Michael Jordan, I was not interested. Then I realized he began to look elsewhere for that companionship and preferred to watch the games with those who shared his interest. At this point, I knew I'd better learn to like this game. I began to watch with him and ask him questions (men really like that). After some time I began to enjoy it because we were bonding simply by my participation in what he was into. The jury is still out on football, but I'm willing to learn because he enjoys it. What is your husband into that you send him off to do on his own? Don't tear down your house by not joining in the things your husband enjoys.

I've heard many stories of women who were "not into what he's into" and lost their husband to another woman. It might not end up in an extramarital affair, but it could be that each time your husband wants to relax, he'd rather call his friends because you won't do anything with him.

SUFFOCATION

While it is important to be a companion to your husband, it is also essential to give him space. Paul has always enjoyed playing basketball and hanging out with his friends. I knew this, but at some point after we married, I changed. I began to resent his times away from home while he was playing basketball. I often made him feel guilty and grudgingly let him go. It wasn't until we had an honest discussion about it that we agreed Monday nights were his time to be with the guys.

Just as every woman needs time with her girlfriends, a man needs guy time.

The foolish woman demands her husband meet her every need. Sometimes we make the mistake of putting our husbands in Jesus' place. I had to learn that I cannot possibly demand my husband listen to my every thought and each detail of my day; I can call my sisters or girlfriends for that. As much as I'd love for him to go shopping with me every time, he cannot fill that need for me. The foolish woman pouts whenever her husband wants to watch sports with other men. This is the suffocating wife, who does not give her husband room to breathe and invest in male relationships.

Now, to avoid unnecessary conflict and suspicions, it's important to discuss and plan time with others. Wife, allow your husband to spend time with other godly men. Don't be foolish by pushing him toward unsaved friends. Sinners sin, and if he is in their company, he may learn their ways:

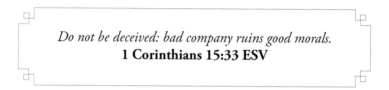

Do not be deceived: bad company ruins good morals.
1 Corinthians 15:33 ESV

This also pertains to family. I heard one woman complain her husband spent too much time with his family and not enough with her. Without knowing the details, I concluded this woman was foremost not connected to her husband's family interactions. Second, it is possible she wasn't creating a safe haven in her home that would cause her husband to want to stay at home. Finally, she was probably demanding he stay home, and the more she did, the more he wanted to stay away, because he might have felt she was pulling him away from the family he had known his entire life.

Wife, what you need to do is to begin building a relationship with his family, showing them love, and even inviting them over. Do not make him choose between you and his family. You can make your home the hangout place by having a welcoming heart.

THE ART OF PLAYING

Learn to *play* with your husband. You're his girlfriend; find that girl your husband fell in love with. Spend time together; plan times when you can just enjoy one another. Don't be serious all the time. Remember what you used to do before you were married and when you were first married. You have to invest in your relationship to keep it healthy. We are all busy, but if we don't stop even for a short time, we may find we now live like roommates with our spouse. Life never stops, but we can stop and take a rest to enjoy one another. Your husband wants the girl he married. Not the mother, grandmother, caregiver, or preacher—just his girl. Get into his world and enjoy it. If he has friends who are not good for him, learn to play with him, and you'll see him prefer to be with you.

I am a rather task-oriented gal, and it's difficult for me to shut down and play with Paul, or even just connect. Paul would often call me just to sit next to him. Not to talk, just to sit and connect with him. I felt it was a waste of time and often fought it—until a light bulb went off: *He just wants to connect with me.* In his world, we were growing closer and connecting. In my world, I had laundry to fold and felt I couldn't afford to sit and do nothing. I had to tell myself the laundry might have to wait. That didn't always work, so I compromised. I sat with Paul when he called for me, but I brought my laundry basket. He was able to connect with me, and I folded my clothes. I think that was pretty smart on my part.

Encourage your husband when he desires to play physically as well. The pat on my behind or the simple grabbing of my breasts while I'm working is connection and play for Paul. If I chide him for doing so, I see his ego deflate and confidence decrease. I have to be careful not to be too serious and ridicule or shun his expressions of affection and play. The play is life-giving to him and to our relationship, so I need to engage in it.

DO YOU BUILD UP OR TEAR DOWN?

A foolish woman refuses to learn what her husband likes and chides him for his desire to play and connect. A wise woman understands her husband's need and joins him in his activities.

DISCUSSION QUESTIONS

1. Why is it important to show interest in your husband's interests?

2. Name three practical ways you can show interest in what your husband is into.

3. What is the definition of a "suffocating wife"?

4. Why does a husband need time with other men?

5. How can you encourage your husband to have time with his family or other men?

6. What is the importance of playing with your husband?

CHAPTER 13

BUT I HAVE NEEDS TOO!

Having the desire to fulfill your husband's needs is in no way submitting yourself to an inferior role as a wife. If you truly love your spouse, then you want to make him happy.
— **Becky Squire**

This quote is powerful because often as wives, we're always looking over the fence to see if our needs are being met at the same level as we're giving. Put simply: *If you start comparing, measuring, weighing your efforts to meet his needs versus his efforts, you will be disappointed.* Not because he isn't putting in any effort but because you've lost sight of what is important, and that is serving your husband and fulfilling his needs. I firmly believe that if husbands and wives spent their time trying to outserve each other, the divorce courts would empty. It's the selfish desire and the 50/50 mentality that drains the energy from the marriage. All the energy you're putting into comparing could be used to find creative ways of meeting your husband's needs. Decide that you are going to do everything you can to fulfill your husband's needs, understanding that you are not inferior to him or a lackey. What you are is a wise woman!

RESPECT

Nevertheless let each one of you in particular so love his own wife as himself, and let the wife see that she respects her husband.
Ephesians 5:33 NKJV

Husbands are to love, and wives are to respect. This Scripture describes our needs in a nutshell. A woman needs and craves love. I believe that although man has the divine nature of God to love, it doesn't come as easily to him. That is why God commanded the husband to love his wife as Christ loves the church. Men, on the other hand, need respect.

Respect to a man is like air, just as love to us is like air. When we are not feeling loved, we start to die on the inside and go into self-preservation mode. This is when we decide, *My needs are not being met, so I need to look out for myself and not depend on or expect my partner to meet my needs.* In looking out for myself and protecting myself, I exhibit certain behaviors such as disrespect, outward dissatisfaction, hurtful words, withdrawing, and withholding love. This is not to give you an excuse to disrespect or to withdraw from your husband, but hopefully, this helps you self-assess when you find yourself dissatisfied with him. If you're not feeling loved, communicate with your husband when you are both relaxed. Don't whine and talk about all his shortcomings, but share with him what fills your love tank.

For example, "I've been feeling uneasy in my heart and realized my love tank needs a refill. I feel energized when you kiss me goodbye or when you tell me how much you enjoyed dinner. I find that when compliments [or whatever it is you need] are few, I start feeling like a fish out of water. You know how to fill my love tank."

This is just an example of how you can communicate your needs, but you know your man best. Don't let the love-tank issue go unresolved, or it will lead to further frustration in your marriage.

Well, the way we need love, the same is true for men. If they don't get the respect they need in order to function, they go into self-preservation mode and begin to withhold love. A foolish woman withholds the good she can give to her mate. The only problem is there could be another woman willing to give him what he is looking for. An important note: it's not that the strange woman is in a competition with the wife, but at the same time, a wife should not give place to the devil.

CROSSING THE THIN LINE

Paul and I pride ourselves on having a great friendship that continues to bind us together. There is, however, a thin line between friendship and respecting your husband. As friends, we can argue and go back and forth, talking freely as friends. There are, however, times when the thin line between husband and friend should not be crossed. I must remember that at the end of the day, he's not only my friend but my husband—my covering and my head.

When I cross the thin line, it's like putting holes in my umbrella and then expecting it to protect me from rain or harsh elements when I need it.

This is exactly what we do as wives when we disrespect and tear down his manhood with our words and actions but get angry when he is not functioning as our head or protection when we need him to. In order to keep the harmony and order God put in place, I must not cross that thin line.

A few years ago, we were on a family vacation in Belize. We were driving one evening with a full van of eight children and six adults, on a narrow, bumpy, curvy road without streetlights. After a few hours, the kids became rowdy. In the midst of the ensuing restlessness, I was playing with the iPad, increasing the rowdiness, and insults began flying as the children started going back and forth with each other over the iPad.

My husband was driving the van and becoming distracted by the noise, which easily could have ended up in an accident. Paul told me to pass him the iPad or to put it away. I refused because I figured he couldn't be serious and felt he was treating me like a child. As his friend, I didn't have to listen to what he had to say; in fact, we went back and forth in the van full of people. I was laughing but did not realize he needed me to honor and respect his voice. Unfortunately, that day I crossed the thin line between friend and husband, and later had to apologize to him and some of the people who had been onlookers. I learned a valuable lesson in a humiliating way. I was the woman in Proverbs 12:4 who shames her husband and is like cancer or rottenness in his bones.

ADMIRATION AND APPRECIATION

You should be your husband's number-one cheerleader, supporter, and encourager. This applies at home and at church. If you're married to a pastor, the way you look at him when he's preaching, showing you're engaged even if you're tired, is special and important to him. Compliment him; tell him you learned something. Admire him in private, and certainly in public. Let your family and friends know you honor your husband as a man of God, even if it may be a matter of calling things that are not as though they were, according to Romans 4:17. Let them know he is a good man and the best husband and father. You teach others how to honor your husband. If you treat him like a little boy, others will do the same. If you treat him like a king, others will do the same. Whenever you're upset by how other people are treating your husband, first ask yourself what kind of attitude and behavior you display toward him. People are watching. Your children are watching.

I particularly like the story of Vashti in the book of Esther:

> *On the seventh day of the feast, when King Xerxes was in high spirits because of the wine, he told the seven eunuchs who attended him—Mehuman, Biztha, Harbona, Bigtha, Abagtha, Zethar, and Carcas—to bring Queen Vashti to him with the royal crown on her head. He wanted the nobles and all the other men to gaze on her beauty, for she was a very beautiful woman. But when they conveyed the king's order to Queen Vashti, she refused to come. This made the king furious, and he burned with anger.*

> *He immediately consulted with his wise advisers,*
> *who knew all the Persian laws and customs, for he*
> *always asked their advice....*
>
> *"What must be done to Queen Vashti?" the king*
> *demanded. "What penalty does the law provide for a*
> *queen who refuses to obey the king's orders, properly*
> *sent through his eunuchs?"*
>
> *Memucan answered the king and his nobles,*
> *"Queen Vashti has wronged not only the king but also*
> *every noble and citizen throughout your empire. Wom-*
> *en everywhere will begin to despise their husbands*
> *when they learn that Queen Vashti has refused to*
> *appear before the king. Before this day is out, the wives*
> *of all the king's nobles throughout Persia and Media*
> *will hear what the queen did and will start treating*
> *their husbands the same way. There will be no end to*
> *their contempt and anger."*
>
> **Esther 1:10–13, 15–18 NLT**

I won't debate whether or not Vashti should have honored the king's request, but the statement his advisors made was powerful. Vashti's treatment of her husband would cause other women to dishonor not only the king but their own husbands as well.

Growing up, my father was always my hero (and he still is), and I truly admired how hard he worked, the spiritual leadership he provided, and how he cared for his family. Though he was often gone, he was still a good father. When I married Paul, I had to fight against comparing him to my father. I would roll my eyes when he told me he was tired and needed to rest. In my mind, you hadn't earned rest until you woke up at three a.m., walked for an hour at six a.m., made it into the office at eight a.m., held several board meetings for major church projects, counseled business owners, received a painful call about a pastor who is not caring for his flock, had evening meetings, and got to bed after eleven p.m. Now, I understand that few people can do this, but in my mind, you only earn rest after working this hard. Paul often laughs about it, saying my father has ruined things for his daughters because our standard for hard work is very high.

In order to show admiration and honor to my husband, I have to put aside the picture of my father and accept Paul for who he is. I have to admire the hours he puts in at work, the spiritual leadership he provides, the time he spends playing with our children. That is what he needs, not a constant comparison to my father.

I find that when I show appreciation and admiration for what he does for the family, it motivates him to work harder.

By contrast, when I'm critical and communicate dissatisfaction with what he does, he's less motivated to work. If you want your husband to work harder, begin to appreciate him for even the smallest things he does. That will boost his ego and give him drive to work and lead his family.

Men's needs are simple: respect, appreciation, and acceptance. As wives, if we become too busy with our lives, businesses, or education and ignore the needs of our husbands, we mess up our marriages. A man wants to feel appreciated and celebrated, not consistently criticized or ignored. Our husbands are constantly communicating to us what they need, and if we meet those needs, there's nothing they would not do for us. Listen to what he talks about. Listen to what he admires in others. Those are usually indicators of his needs.

DO YOU BUILD UP OR TEAR DOWN?
A foolish woman disrespects her husband and does not show him honor, appreciation, and admiration. A wise woman shows respect, admires, and appreciates her husband for even the smallest things he does.

DISCUSSION QUESTIONS

1. Women want to feel loved. What is most important for a husband to feel?

2. What are some ways you can be your husband's number-one cheerleader, supporter, and encourager?

3. Explain the danger of comparing your husband to another man.

4. Have you ever crossed the line between friendship and respecting your husband? How so?

5. Why is friendship important in marriage?

6. Why is Sarah given as an example?

CHAPTER 14

WHAT ABOUT THE JONESES?

Those who bring trouble on their families inherit the wind.
Proverbs 11:29a NLT

I have come to the conclusion that a husband is powerless against a wife who is determined to get what she wants and to have it now. Especially if this woman feels she is in direct competition against the Joneses, who live next door. Of course, what's interesting about this competition is that the Joneses are not aware of, nor are they participating in, the competition.

I have seen many women destroy their homes because they want the big house, the big car, the big ring, etc. I confess that some time ago, I was that woman. Everyone around us seemed to be getting into the real estate business, and I felt we had to get in as well so we wouldn't be left behind. Well, I got my husband into numerous deals that failed, sinking us into debt until we had to foreclose on those properties. All because I was trying to keep up with the Joneses. I thank God our marriage was able to weather that storm, but unfortunately many do not.

We need to do away with unrealistic expectations. If you're both working average-income jobs, don't expect to live high-income lifestyles. Eventually you can work toward an elevated lifestyle, but be realistic. If your mate only has a high school education, don't expect him to be a corporate executive. You knew what he was making or the type of work that he was doing, so when you get married, why do you act surprised that he's not working in the corner office on the top floor? That's not fair to him. How would you feel if you couldn't cook before marriage, but after the honeymoon, your husband expected a five-course meal? Be satisfied with what you have and stop looking over the fence. If you spent as much energy developing yourself and encouraging (not nagging) your husband, your household would be much better off. You should encourage your husband to pursue further education or become more skilled, but don't make him feel less of a man in the process.

Never allow people to pressure you to purchase items you cannot afford; these people are not paying your bills.

One woman I knew was so fixated on having nice things that she opened a credit card without her husband's consent and began charging very expensive items. Her husband was too busy working to notice the packages coming to the door. This wife was so skillful that she had some items delivered to her job, and she'd sneak them into the house and stuff them in the back of the closet. This went on for quite some time until it was time to refinance the house. When the credit report was pulled, there was a credit card that was unfamiliar to the husband, and it had a huge balance—tens of thousands of dollars. He, of course, boldly declared there was an error on the report and said he'd call the credit card to inform them of this error. To his shock, he found out his wife had opened the account. This issue almost brought the marriage to an end, but thank God for a forgiving husband. A foolish woman will jeopardize the financial stability of the home just to keep up with her friends.

Another woman was so desperate to fit in with her new friend that she nagged her husband until he agreed to purchase a home they couldn't afford. Not only did she want this expensive home, she also wanted to be a stay-at-home mom. Needless to say, they didn't remain in that house long. Consequently, the financial pressures further weakened their marriage.

Men are often caught between a rock and a hard place in these situations. The wife demands nice, expensive things without prior planning because she's trying to keep up with the Joneses. And to keep the peace, the husband purchases the things on credit or with the family savings. But when the bills come, the wife somehow forgets that her husband has to work longer hours to pay for those expensive things, and complains he's not spending enough time at home. She makes his life a misery. Dear wife, *what should he do?* You cannot have it both ways!

A wise woman knows how to be satisfied with what her husband can provide, and she adds to the estate. Proverbs 31:16 (NIV), "She considers a field and buys it; out of her earnings she plants a vineyard."

DO YOU BUILD UP OR TEAR DOWN?

A foolish woman spends and is never satisfied and drives her home to poverty, but the wise woman brings wealth into the home and learns to be content.

DISCUSSION QUESTIONS

1. Name three ways wives struggle to keep up with the Joneses.

2. How can you set realistic expectations of your needs?

3. What does it mean that a wife "cannot have it both ways"?

CHAPTER 15

STUPID FEMINISM

The premise of heterophobia is that the feminist mentality shifted from expanding choice for women to an outright visceral and frightening antagonism toward men, wherein heterosexuality itself is to be considered oppressive.
— **Dr. Laura Schlessinger**

L et me begin by stating that this topic is *very* controversial, but I sincerely feel it should be addressed. The dictionary defines feminism as (1) "the belief that women should be allowed the same rights, power, and opportunities as men and be treated in the same way, or the set of activities intended to achieve this state" and (2) "an organized effort to give women the same economic, social, and political rights as men."[10] By this definition, I am a true feminist. I believe in expanding opportunities for women, but I need not be antagonistic toward men to achieve this. But in my opinion, some women have misunderstood true feminism and become misandrists by their efforts to fight for the rights of women. I call this "stupid feminism."

Stupid feminism is killing marriages and unleashing foolish women to tear down their homes in the name of equality.

Stupid feminism can drive us to view our husbands as demanding and unreasonable. I must admit, there are times when I have felt that if Paul and I both work, then why should I be the one following? We cannot have marriages without roles and expect things to work. The husband is to lead, and the wife is to support his leadership, but stupid feminism stands in the way of God's plan for the family.

Your husband wants you to consult with him when making significant decisions that affect the family. Yet society has taught us that we don't need a man; we can do it all by ourselves. We can work to bring the food in the house, cook it and serve it, too. Stupid feminism questions the benefit of serving your husband.

Dr. Laura Schlessinger received this letter from one of her radio show listeners:

> I grew up in the midst of all this "women's lib" nonsense, and actually bought the thought that fathers are not necessary. Though married, I did not stop and think what marriage was really about ... working together. This is an art form I did not learn easily. I thought I was protecting myself and my boys by never depending upon my husband. If he did not see things my way, I did it my way anyway. When he became angry, I would threaten to leave with both boys because "I have already been on my own and could easily do it again."[11]

This woman realized (hopefully not too late) the lie she'd bought into was destroying her marriage and undoubtedly causing great sadness. She called it "nonsense" because it had not paid off for her.

My mother, Dr. Eunor Guti, has lived her life breaking down gender barriers within her African culture. She was the first woman in the nation to become a marriage officiator, which previously was not open to women. In all this, though, she still understands her role as the helper suitable for her husband. She has become a very powerful and accomplished woman in her own right, but I see how she reveres my dad and serves him willingly. I believe this is feminism done well. The woman in Proverbs 31 is another good example of feminism done well. She goes into the marketplace and makes money for her family. Who knows, she may even bring in more money than her husband, but if so, she doesn't seem to hold it against him.

Recent studies have shown that in this new wave of feminism, more women are divorcing their husbands—calling it quits even over chores. I heard one woman say that fights over chores were destroying her marriage, so she hired a cleaning service to save it. That simple decision neutralized the threat. Be careful not to fall into the trap of the enemy, who wants you to see your husband as unreasonable, lazy, and no good. Be extra careful when you earn more money than him; there is temptation to think you are better off without him.

Stupid feminism is destroying manhood. It is destroying the order God has placed in the institution of marriage. It's not *man's* idea for the husband to be the head of the wife; it's *God's* idea. It is also God's idea for husbands and wives to submit to one another. Whenever humanity thinks it has a better idea or we've evolved past God's order, we are setting ourselves up for disaster.

DO YOU BUILD UP OR TEAR DOWN?

A foolish woman is antagonistic toward her husband in the name of equality. A wise woman is a true feminist and understands her role in marriage.

DISCUSSION QUESTIONS

1. How is "stupid feminism" killing marriages?

2. How do you see God's plan for the family in your marriage?

3. Why does a man need to feel needed?

CHAPTER 16

WHAT ABOUT THE CHILDREN?

If you want a one-way ticket to divorce, just put your kids ahead of your spouse. If you end up focusing your attention on kids first, they will consume your world. You will start to resent each other.
— **Mel Robbins**

Children are a heritage and blessing from the Lord. God entrusts us with these precious lives so we can raise them up to be righteous seed for God and to help advance His kingdom against the children of darkness. Children are to be a blessing and not a snare that can destroy homes. Everything has a place, and so do children.

I remember the day I gave birth to our first child, Lydia. It was an incredible feeling, holding a life I'd labored for and brought forth. I cried and cried as I held her for the first time. She was helpless, looking to me for nourishment. Lydia was totally dependent on us. This new life was now our responsibility. When we took her home, we tried to make things as comfortable for her as possible. Paul likes the house cool, but I reminded him he had to consider his daughter and not make it too cool. (Though she dripped sweat from the double layers of clothes I put on her!) Okay, I confess: I often used Lydia's "need" for warmth as an excuse to keep the house temperature to my liking.

As precious and helpless as she was, I'd have been a fool to pay her excessive attention and forget the man who made it possible for me to behold this miracle. It's important to keep the perspective that my relationship with him came before the children and will remain after they leave.

Some parents make the mistake of forgetting that the little ones we sacrifice our relationship for will one day walk away from us. They will not appreciate the fact you didn't pay attention to one another while focusing on their needs, sometimes living vicariously through them. Parents become strangers to each other, forgetting why they married in the first place. No wonder empty-nesters who have not invested in their relationship throughout the child-rearing years often divorce.

The foolish woman puts the children before her mate; she elevates them to the place her husband belongs.

Again, she forgets these children will leave and may even resent her for neglecting the union that brought them into the world. You do your kids a disservice when you make it all about them. This can be an even bigger issue in marriages where the couple struggled with infertility. It's easy for that couple to be focused on this special gift from God and forget "one another." Paul and I often remind our kids that our relationship comes first, and I believe they respect that. We saw this exemplified by our parents who, though empty-nesters, are enjoying one another and growing old together.

When a wife puts the children ahead of her husband, he feels isolated, alone, invisible, and resentful. If you've neglected him for the kids and it seems like he doesn't want you anymore, determine today to begin paying him the attention he's been asking for. Stop the competition between him and the kids. Remember: God first, husband second, children third, and everything else after that.

This issue can be especially challenging in blended families. I know a woman who is right now slowly destroying her home by putting her children ahead of her husband. I have never once heard her mention him in all her years as a married woman. A foolish woman doesn't know her husband longs to be a father to his children, too, not just hers. A wise woman seeks to bring in stepchildren and encourage a healthy relationship with their father.

Some kids know how to pit the parents against each other. In such cases, the mother usually feels like the stepdad doesn't understand because those are not his children. Don't be a fool, especially if the children are grown. Once you remarry, your husband becomes your number-one priority.

HERE ARE SOME IDEAS TO HELP YOU PUT YOUR HUSBAND FIRST:

1. Plan a date night once a week with him. No kids allowed! If you have small children, you may have to be creative—maybe plan a romantic

dinner after they're in bed, or simply have tea or coffee. Put rules in place, including not talking about stressful things during the date night.

2. Find ways to communicate to your husband that he is number one. Ideas include not letting the children interrupt your conversations and reminding them Daddy comes first. Trust me, your kids will learn quickly and begin to respect your quiet time. Plan a getaway for the two of you. This is sure to communicate he is priority. Don't show more excitement when you see your children than your husband. Your husband is always watching, especially if he has felt neglected. It's not because he is weak but because he needs and wants you.

3. Step aside and let your husband participate in parenting of the children. If you take on everything yourself, you'll be frustrated and take it out on your husband. If you think he's not as involved with the kids as you'd like, check to see if you're excluding him from the parenting responsibilities. It is not always him; it might be you.

4. Show your husband kindness and patience as often as you show it to the children. Check your attitude to ensure you are not being kinder to the children than to him.

5. Find and use pet names. Try not to address each other as "Mommy" and "Daddy," especially when the children aren't present.

DO YOU BUILD UP OR TEAR DOWN?
A foolish woman puts children ahead of her husband. A wise woman understands that children have a place, and that is after her husband.

DISCUSSION QUESTIONS

1. What is the place of children within the marriage relationship?

2. What are some ways you can show your husband that he takes priority in your family?

3. What is the danger of always putting the children before your husband?

CHAPTER 17

CHILDHOOD BAGGAGE

For I will restore health to you, and your wounds I will heal, declares the Lord, because they have called you an outcast: "It is Zion, for whom no one cares!"
Jeremiah 30:17 ESV

I t was a weekday evening, and I sat with a young lady in my office who had been married for several years and had several children. She had come to me because she was having difficulty responding to her husband. As we continued to talk about her upbringing, she revealed she had been molested as a child by her father. She's forgiven him but still struggles with receiving affection from men. It is possible for a woman to have sex with her husband but never truly respond to him sexually. Her husband had been very patient but was growing uneasy; he knew he was fighting the ghost of her father. Sadly, issues such as these are all too common in marriages.

Sometimes the ghost that a husband is fighting is that of an ex-spouse or lover. If you have had bad experiences in the past, don't filter your current relationship through the same lens. It is impossible for your husband to compete with a ghost. He is not your former lover. Don't treat him like he is; otherwise, you can destroy your home and lose your husband.

For some, the problems resurface from being raped by a stranger or a visiting family member. For some, it was being fondled at an early age and not understanding what was going on, but now realizing the marriage is being affected.

Some women grow frustrated because the tragic events, which happened so many years ago, still seem to affect how they relate to their spouse. Perhaps they thought they were over the hurt and disappointment, but somehow things keep popping up. This is because memories that were never dealt with are still stored in the subconscious mind. Remember, the enemy who can destroy your home is within you. It might be the trauma you experienced at the hands of someone you trusted and you now have difficulty trusting even your husband.

I want to encourage you to allow the Holy Spirit to heal you so you can experience true joy in your relationship.

> *Beloved, I pray that you may prosper in all things and be in health, just as your soul prospers.*
> **3 John 1:2 NKJV**

It is clear in God's Word that He desires for us to prosper in every area of our life even as our soul prospers. It almost seems to me that as our soul prospers, every other area in our life will prosper.

The health of my soul will dictate the level of prosperity I enjoy in life: in relationships, at work, in my finances, and certainly in my relationship with Christ.

Your emotional health is important to God.

> *The Lord is near to the brokenhearted and saves the crushed in spirit.*
> **Psalm 34:18 ESV**

> *He heals the brokenhearted and binds up their wounds.*
> **Psalm 147:3 ESV**

> *"The Spirit of the Lord God is upon Me, Because the Lord has anointed Me To preach good tidings to the poor; He has sent Me to heal the brokenhearted, To proclaim liberty to the captives, And the opening of the prison to those who are bound; To proclaim the acceptable year of the Lord, And the day of vengeance of our God; To comfort all who mourn, To console those who mourn in Zion, To give them beauty for ashes, The oil of joy for mourning, The garment of praise for the spirit of heaviness; That they may be called trees of righteousness, The planting of the Lord, that He may be glorified."*
> **Isaiah 61:1–3 NKJV**

If you have experienced trauma, know God wants to heal you so you can prosper and be healthy in your marriage. I encourage you to seek counseling so healing can begin. Below are some steps you can take toward emotional health, but remember, healing is a journey, not a one-time event.

SIMPLE KEYS TO EMOTIONAL HEALING

1. **Locate the area of sickness.** Identify the place of sickness or hurt. Ask the Holy Spirit to reveal to you what has been hidden and locked away in your subconscious. Though you are seeing its effects, you may not know what it is. Was it abuse, neglect, lack of secure attachments, living without a safe and loving home, abandonment, hurtful words, etc.? Be honest with yourself once and for all. It is also important to name that pain. When you name something, the healing becomes easier because you know what you are dealing with.

> *Call to me and I will answer you, and will tell you great and hidden things that you have not known.*
> **Jeremiah 33:3 ESV**

As the Holy Spirit reveals to you any buried things, look at those experiences and trauma closely. Don't be quick to brush over it, but allow yourself to experience that moment. Only then can the healing begin.

2. **Grieve the pain.** Acknowledge your hurt. Your experience is valid. Often we invalidate our experiences in hopes of giving them less power over our lives, but they remain stuffed in our subconscious and affect how we do relationship. Grieve the loss of your innocence or your trust, or the violation against your identity or self-esteem. Be aware that sometimes in grieving, we can become angry and experience a myriad of emotions, but allow that process to take place.

3. **Allow Jesus to touch the wound and heal you.** As the Holy Spirit reveals the wounds to you, open them up and ask for the healing balm from Jesus to heal those wounds.

4. **Don't carry what is not yours to carry.**

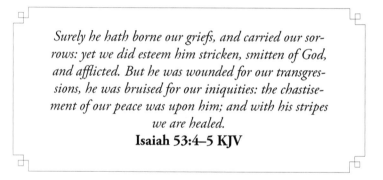

Surely he hath borne our griefs, and carried our sorrows: yet we did esteem him stricken, smitten of God, and afflicted. But he was wounded for our transgressions, he was bruised for our iniquities: the chastisement of our peace was upon him; and with his stripes we are healed.
Isaiah 53:4–5 KJV

Jesus already carried our emotional pain so that we don't have to. You don't have to carry other people's wrongs against you through life. As you grieve the pain, forgive. Forgiving is giving that hurt over to Jesus, because you are not designed to carry it and do not need to try.

5. **Forgive those who have wronged you.** Forgiveness is a choice and a journey. The choice to forgive isn't always easy, but once you make it, you have to walk it out daily, sometimes hourly. The enemy will try to replay the incidents and remind you how they hurt you. Tell him you have forgiven them just as Christ forgave you. You may never be close to the one who hurt you or even have a relationship with

them, but your heart will be clean. You will be able to ask God to forgive you with full confidence He hears you and will do it (Matthew 6:14–15). Don't wait for the wounder to come to themselves and apologize. Forgiveness allows you to retake power from that person. As long as I withhold forgiveness, that person has power over me and control of my destiny. It is only when we release people that we give God permission to deal with them. As long as you hold that person in your heart, God is not able to heal you and deal with them. If they are dead, write a goodbye letter to them, sharing how he/she hurt you and that you have forgiven him/her. This is a good way of bringing closure to the traumatic experience.

6. **Kill the ANTs (Automatic Negative Thoughts).** When we experience trauma, the enemy tries to gain a foothold in our minds and use those experiences for torment. We must challenge and cast down every thought contrary to God's Word (2 Corinthians 10:5). An ANT can be thinking your husband is not trustworthy because he forgot to tell you something. Maybe you automatically think he's cheating on you because your ex-husband did. Challenge every thought that enters your mind. Sometimes it helps to verbalize casting down the imagination or automatic negative thoughts. If you allow ANTs to remain unchallenged, your mind will believe them, and it will affect how you relate to your husband. When you cast down thoughts, you render them powerless over you.

By not dealing with negative or traumatic childhood experiences, a foolish woman destroys her home and pushes her husband away. I strongly advise any woman who has suffered traumatic events to seek help so you can move forward and enjoy your husband.

DO YOU BUILD UP OR TEAR DOWN?
A wise woman recognizes her need for help, but a foolish woman thinks childhood or past experiences do not affect her marriage.

DISCUSSION QUESTIONS

1. How can childhood baggage affect your marriage?

2. How is healing from past trauma possible?

3. How can you include your spouse as you seek help, healing, and restoration?

CHAPTER 18

THE SOCKS ARE ON THE FLOOR AGAIN

> *Catch all the foxes, those little foxes, before they ruin the vineyard of love, for the grapevines are blossoming!*
> **Song of Solomon 2:15 NLT**

It is all those little foxes that spoil the vine. These are the petty issues that result in big arguments—the cause of which we cannot remember a few hours later.

One of my pet peeves is socks and unmentionables on the floor. I don't mind picking up after the kids, but grown folks… Earlier in marriage, I used to lose it because I felt like Paul was treating me like a maid when he left his socks on the floor. Sometimes the hamper was *right next to the socks!* We had many fights—or should I say I lost my temper many times—over these "little foxes."

> *A quarrelsome wife is like the dripping of a leaky roof in a rainstorm.*
> **Proverbs 27:15 NIV**

What happens if the dripping isn't stopped? It will eventually destroy the entire roof.

Petty issues are like constant dripping that, left unresolved, can destroy a good marriage or tear down a home.

A foolish woman refuses to be wronged and wants her mate to suffer. A foolish woman would rather let the socks pile up, in an effort to prove a point, than pick them up herself.

Now, I'm not condoning being silent about things that bother us. Quite the contrary. Utilize your pillow talk with your husband to talk about the small issues that would help you be a better wife. You can say, "It would help me if you'd pick up your socks." Or even, "What would make it easier for you to avoid socks being left on the floor?" If after talking about it you still find socks, pick them up and bring it up at your next talking session. This is wiser than fighting over it—or over the toilet seat left upright, the cupboard doors left open, the baby's diaper not changed properly, etc. Love is not easily angered but endures the test of socks left on the floor (my paraphrase). It takes less effort for me to pick up the socks and go about my business than to show Paul he is wrong and inconsiderate.

> *The very fact that you have lawsuits among you means you have been completely defeated already. Why not rather be wronged? Why not rather be cheated?*
> **1 Corinthians 6:7 NIV**

Why not be wronged? Put the toilet seat down, pick up the socks, fix the bed the way you like it instead of having to be right and causing more strife in the home. Don't give your mate ultimatums; you'll make him feel like a child. This could cause him to resent you or even avoid being around you.

Jay Dixit shared the following in *Psychology Today*…

Irritations are inevitable in relationships. It's just not possible to find another human being whose every quirk, habit, and preference aligns perfectly with yours. The fundamental challenge in a relationship, contends New York psychiatrist John Jacobs, is "figuring out how to negotiate and live with your partner's irritants in a way that doesn't alienate them and keeps the two of you connected." When marriages don't work, he adds, often the partners are fighting not over big issues but over petty differences in style.

We each have differing values and ways of looking at the world, and we want different things from each other. Such differences derive from our genetically influenced temperaments, our belief systems, and experiences growing up in our family of origin, explains Diane Sollee, family therapist and founder of Smart Marriages:

"We think, 'My father knew how to put the toilet seat down, so why can't you?' Or 'My father never put the toilet seat down, so I'm not going to, either.'" Whatever the source, such patterns are deeply ingrained, difficult to dislodge.

Sometimes a sock on the floor is just a sock on the floor. But especially among longtime couples, little irritations may code for deeper problems. It's as if ice cubes become an iceberg, says family therapist John Van Epp. Think of ice cubes as free-floating irritants—bothersome but meaningless: You hate the way your partner puts his feet on the furniture or exaggerates. Such behaviors might drive you up the wall, but they're harmless.

But small problems coalesce into a vast, submerged force when they take on a different meaning in your mind—when you add them up as evidence of a character flaw or moral defect. You're annoyed by the fact that your significant other hates sharing food from her plate. And that she hates planning in advance. And that when you try to share relevant news, she gets excited and cuts you off to share something of her own. When you consider them together, a picture emerges of your partner as selfish and self-absorbed, always putting her own needs first.

"You don't really live with the partner in your home. You live with the partner in your head," explains Van Epp. Gradually, you begin looking for evidence that your partner is self-absorbed— and of course, you find it. Your perceptions shift over time: The idealized partner you started out with becomes, well, less ideal.

But if you want to stay in a relationship, something needs to change. In all likelihood, it's you. Every annoyance in a relationship is really a two-way street. Partners focus on what they're getting, not on what they're giving. But no matter how frustrating a partner's behavior, your interpretation is the greater part of it. What matters is the meaning you attach to it.

The ability to eliminate relationship irritants lies within each of us. They may sabotage good relationships or not. It all depends on how you interpret the problem…. If your partner can't seem to change sloppy ways, reframe the issue in your own mind. Instead of focusing on how inadequately he cleans, remind yourself how much you appreciate his contribution to household chores. Changing your perspective can not only resolve the irritating issue, it can mend the dynamic of the whole relationship.[12]

This statement truly sums it up. We must change; otherwise, we will destroy our marriages.

DO YOU BUILD UP OR TEAR DOWN?

The foolish woman allows petty issues to slowly destroy her marriage. A wise woman is willing to overlook the petty issues and focus on the strength of the marriage as a whole.

DISCUSSION QUESTIONS

1. To what does the phrase "all the little foxes" refer?

2. What are the little foxes in your marriage?

3. How can you extend grace to your husband in the midst of irritations?

CHAPTER 19

SOCIAL-MEDIA TRAP

When unchecked, what begins innocently enough leads to compromise and ultimately to trouble. When it comes to communication with the opposite sex, I believe in open accounts and transparency in conversations.
— Dr. David Hawkins

Facebook and other social-media avenues are destroying marriages. I've heard countless stories of how a simple click to confirm or invite a friend has led to the breakdown of marriages. I know of a wife who, in a moment of weakness, decided to search for her high school sweetheart just to see how he was doing. She found out he was unhappy in his marriage. She was bored in *her* marriage and wanted a little excitement. What began as a seemingly innocent conversation led to an emotional affair, and eventually a sexual one. With the click of a button, her marriage was destroyed.

Steven Kimmons, Ph.D., of Loyola University Medical Center in Maywood, Ill., describes one way such extramarital relationships start.

"One spouse connects online with someone they knew from high school. The person is emotionally available, and they start communicating through Facebook," Kimmons explains. "Within a short amount of time, the sharing of personal stories can lead to a deepened sense of intimacy, which in turn can point the couple in the direction of physical contact."

An errant spouse may not set out to do wrong. The person may simply be curious about what an old friend or an old flame is doing and decide to say "hello" online, Kimmons says. If the errant spouse ends up talking to the old friend more often than their own spouse, "you don't need a fancy psychological study to conclude that I'm more likely to fall in love with the person I talk to five times a week because I have more contact with that person," he says. The beginning of such a relationship may be innocent, but its continuation is not.

In the same article, Mark Gaither, founder of Redemptive Heart Ministries, puts it this way:

"In general, cheating is the wayward partner's attempt to get needs met outside the marriage. That's not to say the cheater's spouse is necessarily neglectful or blameworthy. Every married individual has faults or flaws."

He describes this kind of behavior as "a symptom of the wayward spouse's choice to misbehave rather than address issues in the marriage or face deep, personal issues."

"Social networking and online dating sites make this option easier," says Gaither. "Even if a cyber-relationship doesn't result in physical contact, a dissatisfied partner can undermine the marriage by engaging in an emotional affair instead of working through issues in the marriage."[13]

A wife needs to be careful not to have private conversations with other men, especially in the inbox.

It has now become easier to connect with an old flame from high school and begin an emotional, which could lead to a physical, affair.

A wise woman will encourage her husband not to get into lengthy conversations with other women, even if they are seeking help. In addition to social media, the Internet as a whole has become a tool the enemy uses to destroy marriages. Have an open policy in passwords. Your husband should be able to log in to your social-media accounts and have access to all your business. Your business is his business and vice versa. Accountability is important and a protective factor. If you or your spouse is very protective over account access, you are simply giving the devil a foothold in your marriage. If this is happening in your marriage, the stage is set for infidelity. Seek counseling if you and your spouse are not able to agree on this because you want to close doors to infidelity.

While on this matter, let's talk about wives having men for close friends. This spells disaster! My daughter recently asked me if a guy and a girl can be friends. Not for too long, I told her; someone will eventually develop feelings for the other. My fellow sister, if you are in a close relationship with another man than your husband, you need to create distance. If you find yourself looking forward to sharing your intimate secrets with another man, you are in trouble. Don't confide in another man, especially regarding your marriage. It's a trap designed to destroy your marriage. If you're attracted to this friend, cut off the relationship and seek counseling before you mess up your marriage, especially if you have developed an emotional connection.

DO YOU BUILD UP OR TEAR DOWN?

A foolish woman has secret conversations online with other men. A wise woman is open with her communications with other men and allows her husband access to all communication accounts.

DISCUSSION QUESTIONS

1. What potential temptations lie within social media?

2. What are some safeguards to put in place for social-media management within marriage?

3. If you haven't already, have a discussion of online boundaries with your husband. Be sure to share all passwords and usernames.

CHAPTER 20

KEEPING UP APPEARANCES

A wife who doesn't keep up her appearance is taking her husband's attraction to her for granted and communicates she doesn't care for his affection.
— **Paul Arthurs**

Men are visual creatures. They desire and appreciate beauty. Every man wants his wife to look good for him, even if he may not know exactly what he wants until he sees it. When some of us were waiting to be found, we worked hard on looking good, but after we were found, we let ourselves go. Some of our husbands have to work with very attractive women and then come home to us looking like an old grandmother. This can tempt your husband to start fantasizing about what it would be like to be with that woman at work. A foolish woman figures she has the man and he should love her the way she is. Reality check: he will still love you but not be attracted to you.

In *What He Is Not Telling You*, David Murrow writes:

What's going through your mind when you see a goddess out in public? Most of the time my thoughts are benign. I'm simply admiring a beautiful woman. I'm not imagining myself in bed with her. I'm just enjoying the pleasure of observing something beautiful—much as I would enjoy looking at a sunset, a work of art, or a fine automobile. But the pleasure of spotting a beautiful woman is more primal and intense because it's linked to the survival of the human race.[14]

This is true, and a wise woman will heed it. Recently, our family was on vacation at the beach. It was very hot, so I ran into the water for a quick cool-down. When I came back to Paul, he mentioned having spotted a beauty walking by who looked ready for the beach. A few minutes later she passed us again, and Paul pointed her out to me. Yes, she certainly was a beauty, with curves all in the right places. We had a good laugh about it when I told him *that* body hadn't been through anything like three pregnancies—my curves have been tried and tested! The point is, it's natural for men to spot beauty because they are visual. A wise woman does herself a favor by caring for her body and keeping it well groomed.

As I mentioned earlier, some men don't know what they want until they see it. Try different hairstyles, clothing styles, makeup, etc., until he tells you what he likes. Remember, you should dress for him first and not for other people. My husband was one of those men who insisted on little or no makeup on principle. I went along with it for a while, but I realized my skin tone needed to be evened out, so I started wearing a little makeup, and he ended up liking it. I think makeup gets a bad rap with men because some women pile it on so thick they don't look like themselves.

A woman with low self-esteem is a turnoff to her husband.

It is the husband's role to cultivate her to be the woman God intends her to be. A woman must be saturated in the Word to know who she is and that she is made in His image. A man wants a confident woman, and her attire has a lot to do with her confidence. I've found that when I am properly groomed and looking my best (no matter my dress size), I am more confident (and, frankly, more of a joy to be around). Perhaps you are like me and don't have a good sense of fashion. Do what I do and enlist those with that natural ability to help.

It's okay to accentuate your positives. If you need to, get help to create a beautiful, natural look for yourself. Makeup is only to enhance beauty, not make you into someone else. Find someone to help with your hair as well. I recommend starting a small group of women to help each other along these lines. But remember, you are dressing for your husband first, not to please other women.

My dear father-in-law, Pastor Carlton Arthurs, always tells women to do whatever they can to help the cause, to enhance the raw material and increase attractiveness. Our church recently had a small group to teach women how to apply makeup, use hair care, and select a wardrobe. I attended the class because I'm always on a mission to keep Paul Arthurs into me. I do not take his love and desire for attractiveness for granted.

DO YOU BUILD UP OR TEAR DOWN?

A foolish woman neglects caring for herself, forgetting her husband is visually stimulated. A wise woman does all she can to keep her husband visually stimulated and attracted to her.

DISCUSSION QUESTIONS

1. Why should a married woman be concerned about her appearance?

2. Along with attire, what else makes a woman attractive to her husband?

3. What women of your acquaintance might be interested in forming a group where women with gifts in fashion and aesthetics could share?

CHAPTER 21

NOT TONIGHT, DEAR

> *Do not deprive each other of sexual relations, unless you both agree to refrain from sexual intimacy for a limited time so you can give yourselves more completely to prayer. Afterward, you should come together again so that Satan won't be able to tempt you because of your lack of self-control.*
> **1 Corinthians 7:5 NLT**

I am amazed that the very thing we get married for (besides companionship and security) is the thing that produces so much stress in marriage. The foolish woman denies her husband the thing he married her for. If husbands got a dollar for every time wives say, "Not tonight, dear, I have a headache; I'm too tired, I'm not in the mood," many would be millionaires!

While writing this book I encountered a study by a female gynecologist that concluded—are you ready for it? You may want to hide this part from your husband (just kidding)—*sex can help cure some headaches!* Can you believe it? If a *male* doctor had said this, I'd have quickly dismissed it, but a *female* doctor conducted a study of a few hundred ladies. There are numerous studies on this, so do your own research if you don't believe me.

Wait! Don't put the book down yet—keep reading! The study says some headaches are cured, but not all. Yes, headaches are real and do occur more frequently for some.

There are sometimes legitimate reasons why a wife may say she has a headache or sickness as an excuse not to have sex:

• Tiredness

• Illness

• Medication

- Unhealthy lifestyle

- Pain during sex. If this is your issue, talk to your gynecologist. There is likely something that can be done about it.

- Unresolved conflict. It is difficult for you to open yourself up to your husband if you are angry or disappointed with him and you haven't talked about it.

- No sexual enjoyment—whenever sex does occur, the husband gets on, gets in, deposits, and gets off. Sisters, I agree this does not make for mutually satisfying sex and can cause you to dread your husband touching you. Many wives have been left empty, feeling used because the husband does not take time to stimulate her or to learn to control his ejaculation.

- Past negative sexual experiences

- Comparing the spouse with former lovers

- Lack of communication about each other's needs

Your husband cannot possibly guess what you want, how you like to be touched, what hurts, what doesn't feel good. He is not omniscient. Talk to him.

Next time you're tempted to say, "Not tonight, dear, I have a headache," consider what sex means to him and what it can do for you both.

WHAT EVERY WIFE NEEDS TO KNOW ABOUT SEX AND HER HUSBAND:

1. Sex feels good and is good for you. Sex has been recorded to have great physiological and psychological benefits, in particular penile-vaginal intercourse.[15] Both men and women receive health benefits, which include lower blood pressure, sustainable sex drive, and lower stress levels. Plus, it helps the vaginal wall maintain its strength, thus reducing pain during intercourse, and it may lower the risk of prostate cancer.

2. Ejaculation is a normal function and need for men. God designed men to produce sperm, and they have to ejaculate every so often. It's

part of nature. This may manifest itself as though all the man wants is sex, but in reality he is simply satisfying his sex drive God gave him. The reason humans want sex is due to testosterone, a predominantly male hormone. A normal male's body produces twenty times more of this hormone than a female's.

- In other words, a male feels the same way after one day without sex as a female after twenty days without sex. A male who has not had sex in twenty days feels the same way as a female after more than a year without sex.

3. Foreplay for the man is meant to lead to sexual intercourse. Men don't usually just want to hold the wife like we sometimes want; they want the full course.

4. Sex makes him feel loved and desired. Every man has a desire for his wife to want him and desire him and his body. If you don't, this could send him into a depression.

5. Sex, good sex, boosts a man's ego. The sex drive is linked to his ego. A sexually satisfied man has a better self-esteem.

6. A man's performance is tied to his sexual life. If sex is not happening, the man's self-esteem is affected. He will not perform as well on his job, in the home, or in life in general.

A man becomes sheepish and withdrawn because the thing that helps make him a man is denied him.

---

7. Sex is a great stress-reliever for men. Sex reduces friction in the home. A sexually satisfied male is happier even when very little is going well for him. Sexually dissatisfied men are irritable and snap at both the wife and children. Men use sex for tension relief. Don't be offended; be a willing participant in relieving his stress. When you do that, his head is clearer and able to bring solutions.

8. Sex is visual. Your husband may want to have sex with the lights on sometimes. It's how he is wired.

In the book *The Proper Care and Feeding of Marriage*, Dr. Schlessinger shared a reader's comment:

> My wife informed me earlier this year that she just doesn't have any interest in sex anymore (she is 36 and I am 40). I can't remember a time of intimacy in the last 5 years that she didn't make me feel that she was "allowing" me to have "make it quick" sex with her, and without making me feel pathetic about the urge. Her refusal to do anything at all that she doesn't "feel" like doing has robbed me of all the joy in my life, both in marriage and motivation for work. It is affecting my children in that they don't get the chance to see love and affection between their parents.[16]

What an amazing blessing it must be for men who have wives who actually contemplate their husbands' feelings and think about doing the simple things that make a man feel like a man.

Another man in the same book said:

> I am drudging through a day at a time, hoping that when my daughters are grown and out, that I will still have the energy and desire to go out and find someone with who I might share my joy, achievements, and affection, that's the only hope for a man who will never spend a single day away from girls as they grow, and who has a wife that says, "get over it, you are married ... go take care of yourself in the shower."

Wow, what a foolish woman indeed, to tell her husband to go masturbate because she is not willing to perform her wifely duties!

WAYS TO KICK-START OR IMPROVE YOUR SEX LIFE:

1. Pray and ask God to give you a desire to meet your husband's needs and to reveal to you what happens to your relationship when you constantly decline to have sex.

2. Create an atmosphere that is conducive for lovemaking. A clean room helps, as do clean sheets on the bed. A nice, hot evening shower might even help. Sex is largely emotional and mental for women, so create an atmosphere that gets you in the mood. Don't wait for your husband to do it for you. There is something we can learn from the adulteress:

> *So she caught him and kissed him; With an impudent*
> *face she said to him: "I have peace offerings with me;*
> *Today I have paid my vows. So I came out to meet you,*
> *Diligently to seek your face, And I have found you. I*
> *have spread my bed with tapestry, Colored coverings*
> *of Egyptian linen. I have perfumed my bed with myrrh,*
> *aloes, and cinnamon. Come, let us take our fill of love*
> *until morning; Let us delight ourselves with love."…*
> *With her enticing speech she caused him to yield, With*
> *her flattering lips she seduced him.*
> **Proverbs 7:13–18, 21 NKJV**

3. Communicate your needs. If you do not usually reach an orgasm, tell your husband, but not during intercourse. Wait until you are not necessarily about to have sex, but maybe just during pillow talk. Tell him in such a way that his self-esteem is not shattered. Every man wants to know he can sexually fulfill his wife. If he finds out otherwise, he may become defensive, blame the wife for not participating, or become sheepish in approaching her for sex. During the sexual act, you can simply guide him to areas that are stimulating you that day. He's not a mind-reader, so eliminate frustration by guiding and directing gently with your hands. It is important to note that not every woman reaches orgasm in intercourse. You might fall in that percentage of women who have to be stimulated to orgasm.

4. Take responsibility for your pleasure. Some women just lie there and expect the husband to do all the work. No, participate. Get your mind into it and your body will respond. Sex begins in the mind, so when you can focus and not make a grocery list during sex, chances are you will be more fulfilled. Go for your satisfaction and pleasure without hesitation. I bet you your husband is going for his pleasure while you are busy complaining in your mind. A wise woman should not complain that her husband doesn't slow down for her or make sure she is satisfied. Slow him down, tell him you want him to take his time because you know it's important to him that you are sexually fulfilled. Sex is not just for the man but for you too. Just the same way your body belongs to your husband, his body belongs to you, so use it for your pleasure as it was designed.

Sex is not something that happens to you. Sex is something that you engage in.

5. Study what your husband likes and needs. Be aware of his erection during foreplay. Working to keep it strong will enable him to pleasure you even more.

6. If you are truly unable to engage for valid reasons, make sure you give an EDS (Expected Date for Sex), but use it sparingly, only under extenuating circumstances. The conversation can go something like this: "It is my desire to please you and to be available for you, but right now I am not feeling well at all. I've spread myself thin and will do something to change my schedule so I can be available to make love with you."

7. Make an appointment to have sex if you are not finding enough time in your schedule, but don't make scheduling a habit.

8. Evaluate your reasons for the headaches and see what changes can be made:

    • Slow down a little

    • Learn to say no to things that might tire you out

    • Manage your time wisely

    • Be healthy—eat right, exercise, and get some rest

    • Seek counseling for some issues you might have had in the past

9. Accept his playful advances; don't shut him down. Don't rebuke him for wanting to touch you outside the bed. You can't have it both ways, complaining he only touches you in bed and on the flip side rebuking him for fondling your breasts while you're cooking.

10. Get the baby out of the bed as soon as possible. The baby will survive in the crib. There is no romance-drainer like a child in the bed.

11. Thank him for sex. Tell him that no one else satisfies you as he does. He wants to know that you desire him, that he is a good lover.

12. Be spontaneous. Dress in lingerie. Come to bed nude. When I see

my husband stressed or under pressure, I undress in front of him and walk around nude. Build up expectations for him by stating what you intend to do to him and how you're going to make his worries go away, at least temporarily. Don't be reserved or too "holy." Make noise if possible to indicate he is pleasuring you. This too will give him confidence knowing he is pleasuring his wife. Be willing to try sex in different places. You have all the tools you need to satisfy your husband.

13. Take care of business before you or your husband leave on a trip. Leave a memory with him that will carry him through the days away from you. While you are apart, talk to each other about what your reunion will be like, what you plan on doing to each other. I'll leave it at that, but the point is made.

14. If you have been abused and find it difficult to engage and enjoy sex, seek counseling so you can heal. On this note, it is important for women (and men too) to be honest about their past, especially if it is likely to interfere with the sex life. Marriages are sometimes destroyed simply because some issues were never exposed and healed. Don't live frustrated and certainly don't leave your husband to live in frustration and baffled at what he has done wrong. Be honest and get healing.

Dr. Kevin Leman shared the following in his book *7 Things He'll Never Tell You*:

Guess what, ladies? Your husband wants you to take care of yourself, but those few extra pounds on the hips and thighs and having small breasts don't matter to your man. What he wants is a willing woman in bed. Being a willing wife will take pounds off your figure (or add them in the right places!) and make you look even more attractive to your husband.[17]

DO YOU BUILD UP OR TEAR DOWN?
A foolish woman does not render due benevolence to her husband. A wise woman is a doer of the word by rendering the benevolence that is due to her husband.

DISCUSSION QUESTIONS

1. What leads to your own lack of sexual intimacy?

2. Why do men crave sexual intimacy?

3. Have an honest conversation with your husband about your sex life. Ask him to tell you what he enjoys, and let him know what you like or do not like as well.

4. Share a sexual fantasy you have with your husband and ask him to share his.

CHAPTER 22

IN-LAW INTERFERENCE

> *A man leaves his father and mother and is joined to*
> *his wife, and the two are united into one.*
> **Ephesians 5:31 NLT**

A foolish woman tears down her house and messes up her marriage by putting her family before her spouse. She allows her family to interfere in her home. She lets her family speak ill of her husband and of the decisions made in the home. She brings opinions from her family of origin into the decision-making process. This woman forgets that when she said "I do," her allegiance should have changed from family to husband. Furthermore, she divulges behind-closed-doors conversations to her family, who then begin to view her husband negatively. The interference tends to intensify unless it is cut off.

I thank God for a wonderful mother-in-law. Due to overcoming her experiences with her in-laws, she is a blessing in my life. When she sees issues in our marriage, she talks to me, not to Paul, thus averting tension in our home. My parents always challenge me to see Paul's side of matters because they understand the importance of not interfering in our marriage by taking my side.

I know of a wise woman who, before marriage, was the backbone of her family financially and emotionally. Early in her marriage the family came to her as usual with their issues. She was wise enough to allow her husband to communicate directly with her family on these matters. A foolish woman would have kept things going as usual and helped her family directly. I know of some instances where the woman has buckled under her family's never-ending needs and secretly sent money to them. She didn't realize that what she was doing was actually destroying her home.

Ephesians 6:1 tells us to honor our father and mother, but to cleave to our spouse—not our parents. This explains why a man leaves his father and mother and is joined to his wife, and the two are united into one (Genesis 2:24 NLT).

I recommend couples discuss the extent of their support for either family prior to marriage to avoid contention. If consistent financial help is needed, there should be an agreement on the maximum amount based on the budget. If you have been giving support to your family behind your husband's back, make the commitment to change. Next time your family asks for support of any kind, tell them that you have to clear any support with your husband. It might be difficult to do a course correction with your family and establish good boundaries, but it is worth it.

If you have been speaking negatively about your husband to your family, put a halt to that behavior immediately. When your family says something negative about your husband, counter the negativity with positive traits about your husband. They may not get the message at first, but they will eventually see that you are not that foolish woman. If the opportunity arises, you can repent before your family for undressing your husband in conversation with them and say that now you realize what a good man you have.

Wives can mess up their marriage by having an antagonistic relationship with their in-laws.

A wife needs to remember that though she comes first, her husband is forever connected to his family.

A foolish wife prevents her husband from remaining connected to his family. By doing this, she puts her husband in a position to have to choose between her and his family. This is hardly fair to him. Instead of fighting an ugly, hurtful, and losing battle, it is better to join him. You can't beat the love your husband has for his family, so join him in loving them. Work at winning his family, beginning with his mother and sisters. Even if they've offended you, determine to not only love them inwardly but to *show* them love. If your in-laws are expecting you to be mean or to show contempt, throw them off and shake things up by doing the complete opposite according to Proverbs 25:21 and 22. Verse 22 ends with "And the Lord will reward you." When you do your part to show love in spite of how your in-laws treat you, God will reward you. Find creative ways to communicate you love them. Show respect and love to his family, and you'll win him over. As a wife, you have to love what he loves. That's true partnership in marriage.

DO YOU BUILD UP OR TEAR DOWN?

A foolish woman allows her family to interfere in her marriage, causing discord and tension. A wise woman puts her family in their place—outside the marriage.

DISCUSSION QUESTIONS

1. How do you set boundaries for what conversations need to remain behind closed doors?

2. How can you honor your parents and still cleave to your spouse?

3. Who in your husband's family of origin would benefit from your extending extra grace in the relationship?

CHAPTER 23

WHERE'S THE WIFE?

Some time ago, Paul and I were driving with one of my sisters-in-law, talking about people, particularly one man, getting into heresy. In the midst of the discussion, my sister-in-law asked, "Where was the wife when he came up with this nonsense? That should have been taken care of in the bedroom before he came out with that." This caught my attention because a wise woman does help her husband and should be the first line of defense when he is going into strange teaching.

In my lifetime I've come across many women who, in the name of submission, foolishly followed their husbands by leaving their places and people that helped forge their spiritual identity. I've also met wise women who refused to go along with what they knew was wrong, unethical, and heretical. As women, we have God-given intuition or discernment we need to use to help our husbands.

The two women I want to highlight are Sapphira and Pontius Pilate's wife. Sapphira, found in Acts, is a classic example of a woman who followed blindly. Her husband wanted to keep some of the money they were giving in offering. She should have quickly shut down that idea in the bedroom.

> *But a certain man named Ananias, with Sapphira his wife, sold a possession. And he kept back part of the proceeds, his wife also being aware of it, and brought a certain part and laid it at the apostles' feet. But Peter said, "Ananias, why has Satan filled your heart to lie to the Holy Spirit and keep back part of the price of the land for yourself? While it remained, was it not your own? And after it was sold, was it not in your own control? Why have you conceived this thing in your heart? You have not lied to men but to God."*
> **Acts 5:1–4 NKJV**

Sapphira represented a foolish woman who didn't protect her husband, was not sensitive to the Holy Spirit, and was most likely not a praying woman. She knew their intended deceit was wrong, but she went along with it. What a foolish woman! It cost her life. For most foolish women, the result may not be physical death but spiritual death, wandering, poverty, and a life of struggle.

Conversely, Pontius Pilate's wife (whose name the Bible does not mention) was a wise woman who kept her husband out of trouble.

> *Now Jesus stood before the governor. And the governor asked Him, saying, "Are You the King of the Jews?"*
>
> *Jesus said to him, "It is as you say." And while He was being accused by the chief priests and elders, He answered nothing.*
>
> *Then Pilate said to Him, "Do You not hear how many things they testify against You?" But He answered him not one word, so that the governor marveled greatly.*
>
> *Now at the feast the governor was accustomed to releasing to the multitude one prisoner whom they wished. And at that time they had a notorious prisoner called Barabbas. Therefore, when they had gathered together, Pilate said to them, "Whom do you want me to release to you? Barabbas, or Jesus who is called Christ?" For he knew that they had handed Him over because of envy.*
>
> *While he was sitting on the judgment seat, his wife sent to him, saying, "Have nothing to do with that just Man, for I have suffered many things today in a dream because of Him."*
> **Matthew 27:11–19 NKJV**

> *When Pilate saw that he could not prevail at all, but rather that a tumult was rising, he took water and washed his hands before the multitude, saying, "I am innocent of the blood of this just Person. You see to it."*
> **Matthew 27:24 NKJV**

A few things strike me in these passages. Mrs. Pilate must have been a sensible woman for her husband to listen to her. I don't believe she was clamorous and loud (Proverbs 7:11). I believe she was spiritually sensitive and discerning. Her husband's heart must have safely trusted in her, or he would have simply dismissed her warning.

> *The heart of her husband safely trusts her; So he will*
> *have no lack of gain. She does him good and not evil*
> *All the days of her life.*
> **Proverbs 31:11–12 NKJV**

She must have been a woman who built her house and who spoke few words, but words filled with sound judgment.

> *She opens her mouth with wisdom, And on her tongue*
> *is the law of kindness.*
> **Proverbs 31:26 NKJV**

Pilate's wife wasn't afraid to tell her husband the truth, but in a respectful way. Her personal ambitions did not blind her to the danger her husband was walking into. Some wives are aware their husband is going off in the wrong direction, but choose to overlook it, if that direction promises lights and glamour. Not so with Mrs. Pilate. It appears it was more important to her to protect her husband than to be popular with the Jews.

> *[Haman's] wife Zeresh and all his friends said to him,*
> *"Have a pole set up, reaching to a height of fifty cubits,*
> *and ask the king in the morning to have Mordecai*
> *impaled on it. Then go with the king to the banquet*
> *and enjoy yourself." This suggestion delighted Haman,*
> *and he had the pole set up.*
> **Esther 5:14 NIV**

Haman's wife seemed to have been the one leading the suggestion to hang Mordecai. I believe she was so blinded by her own ambitions as well as her desire to see her husband happy. Dear wife, make sure you are the voice of reason in your husband's life, and do not get caught up in fighting his wars for him. Zeresh probably saw the distress her husband was experiencing and felt the urge to do something about it, neglecting her role to speak wisdom.

THE WISE WOMAN HELPS HER HUSBAND:

1. **In prayer.** She does this by encouraging him to be the priest in the home and does not compete with him. She has intimate fellowship with God, and He tells her secrets (Psalm 25:14), which she then shares with her husband. Needless to say, the wise woman shares with humility and wisdom so her husband accepts her input. For example, rather than saying, "God told me so-and-so," a better way may be to say, "While praying I sensed…" or, "I feel the Lord is saying…" It takes time to build that trust, so don't be discouraged.

2. **To limit making mistakes/bad judgments.** Sometimes you can't prevent your husband from making mistakes, but at least voice your concern and certainly pray. If your family is going to be without a roof over their head because of a bad decision your husband is about to make, be wise and put something aside. I can assure you he will thank you someday for being proactive and not stupidly submitting. Abigail is a great example of this. She knew she was married to a fool and had to be proactive in order to save her family (1 Samuel 25:1–38).

3. **In basic grooming.** This includes bad breath and body odor. I'm always surprised at both men and women who don't share with their partners about such matters. It's like everyone but the couple is aware. I often carry breath strips, and if I'm not in a position to discreetly tell Paul he needs to freshen his breath, I simply offer him one. There are times when he declines, but then I gently tell him he needs one. I, of course, expect the same treatment because we are to help each other. My husband now knows when I offer him a breath mint, it's because I'm helping him. My fellow sister, it is perfectly acceptable to communicate these things with your mate so people do not avoid him. That's a wise woman.

4. **In maintaining sexual purity.** In this day and age of Internet and easily accessible sexual content, every wife needs wisdom in knowing how to protect her husband. I trust my husband, but not the devil.

Take this seriously and explore with your husband to put safeguards in place. Things like passwords to email and social-media accounts, etc., should be known by both parties. Covenant Eyes (www.CovenantEyes.com) is an Internet accountability and filtering system that can be helpful in maintaining sexual purity.

5. **In ministry development.** This may be directed more to pastors' wives and much of which is beyond the scope of this book. One particular point I'd highlight is when he is preaching. If you know your husband tends to go overtime, discuss behind closed doors and suggest ways you can help him know his time is up. One way that works when Paul is out preaching is for me to hold pieces of paper (discreetly, of course) counting down from ten minutes to zero. Find what works for you both, but be a wise woman and help your husband so people can be relaxed, knowing he respects the time given. You can also help him by purchasing books for him that can be beneficial in his ministry development.

DO YOU BUILD UP OR TEAR DOWN?
A foolish woman neglects her responsibility to protect her husband. A wise woman is sober, vigilant, and unafraid to respectfully challenge her husband and protect him.

DISCUSSION QUESTIONS

1. Share a time when you had to stand up for what was right in the face of opposition from your husband.

2. Judging by his reaction, how did Pontius Pilate feel about his wife? Why?

3. List three practical ways you can look out for and help your husband.

CHAPTER 24

THE JOURNEY CONTINUES

Now that you know some foolish things wives do to mess up their marriages, what's next? I encourage you to make a commitment to be a wise woman who builds. As you go on this journey, you may fall or do things that mess up your marriage, but don't lose heart. You are on a lifelong journey. A wise woman does indeed build her house, and every woman has in her the ability to be wise through Jesus Christ. We've all made foolish mistakes, and I have played the chief foolish woman, but through God's grace I can rebuild my house. Do not beat yourself down, but see what you can take away and implement in your life. The power is in your hands to make your home what it should be. Yes, it takes two to build a strong marriage, but God has given us strong influence in the building process. Let's use it for His glory.

I would also like to add a word of encouragement to the wife who is living in a loveless marriage. Maybe you feel like it's too late or there has been too much damage, and you are ready to quit. I urge you to look to the Lord and do not lose hope. Earlier I talked about the power of prayer. As long as there is breath in your body and your husband's body, there is hope. I am not promising a quick fix, but I have seen dead relationships come back to life when hope was kept alive. Sometimes the change is as simple as peace instead of turmoil in the storm. God is faithful and well able.

This is my prayer for you and me:

> *I pray that your love [for God, for your husband] will overflow more and more, and that you will keep on growing in knowledge and understanding [of God and of your husband]. For I want you to understand what really matters, so that you may live pure and blameless lives until the day of Christ's return. May you always be filled with the fruit of your salvation—the righteous character produced in your life by Jesus Christ—for this will bring much glory and praise to God.*
> **Philippians 1:9–11 NLT**

You are a wise woman who builds, not one who destroys her home!

If you have not made Jesus Christ the Lord of your life or if you have been following from afar, I want to invite you to commit or recommit your life to the Lord. You cannot even begin to build a healthy marriage without a relationship with Christ.

> *Heavenly Father, thank you for sending Your only Son to die for my sin. I believe that You died, that You were buried, and that You rose again from the dead and that You are the very Son of the living God. I open my heart and receive You as my Lord and Savior. Forgive me for all of my sin. I renounce the devil and all his works, and I boldly declare You are Lord of my life. Thank you, Lord, for saving me, making me a citizen of Your kingdom, and allowing me to spend eternity with You.*

If you prayed that prayer, allow me to be the first to welcome you into the family. You are "a new creation in Christ Jesus; old things have passed away; behold, all things have become new" (2 Corinthians 5:17). You might not hear angels singing, see rainbows, or feel goose bumps, but you are a child of God. I encourage you to take the next step and find a church that believes and teaches the Bible, and tell them you recently accepted Christ. I also would love to hear from you and send you some material to help you grow in your walk with God. Feel free to send me an email at *hello@paulandfiona.org*.

FOOLISHNESS ASSESSMENT

(Note: This is not a scientific assessment.)

PUT A CHECK BY EACH STATEMENT THAT IS A "YES."

1. I do not accept my responsibility for the health and state of my marriage.

2. I do not understand my role as the builder of my home.

3. I am not consistent in my personal devotions with God.

4. I do not pray for my marriage on a regular basis.

5. I honestly do not have a positive outlook on my marriage.

6. I have doubts that my husband is God's gift to me.

7. I find myself secretly wishing I had married someone else.

8. I find it difficult to let it go when my husband wrongs me.

9. I often have to nag my husband to get him to do things around the house.

10. My husband tends to make excuses for coming home late.

11. I often find myself looking at my husband with contempt/disgust.

12. I do not always use words that build up my husband.

13. I have difficulty following my husband's leadership.

14. I have not shown my in-laws an act of kindness recently.

15. I decline my husband's sexual advances more often than not.

16. My husband does not satisfy me sexually.

17. I rarely communicate appreciation to my husband.

18. I am not a good steward of our household finances.

19. I don't see the point in making an effort with my physical appearance.

20. I have given up hope because I have tried but he did not change.

ADD UP THE TOTAL NUMBER OF CHECKMARKS TO DETERMINE YOUR FOOLISHNESS SEVERITY:

0–4   Little to no foolishness detected, but keep working on it!

5–9   Next stop, foolishness, so be careful!

10–20 Yep—you are foolish—but there is hope!

ABOUT THE AUTHOR

Fiona Arthurs was born and raised in Zimbabwe, Africa. She married her love, Paul, in 1996. Fiona has a passion to see women fulfilled through discovering their identity and role as women of God. She desires to see marriages and family relationships restored in these days when families are under a great attack. Fiona has served in women's ministry for over twenty years. She brings a wealth of experience and a broad cultural perspective from which she extracts biblical principles for daily living. Fiona's transparent and girl-next-door approach makes her a great speaker at churches, women's events, and marriage retreats.

Fiona holds a master's in marriage and family therapy from Wheaton College and is a licensed marriage and family therapist. Paul and Fiona are co-founders of The Carlton Center, a nonprofit, faith-based organization designed to uplift and enhance the quality of life and relationships for youth and their families. They believe families should live a better story and have healthier generational relational patterns.

Fiona is the proud mother of three children: Lydia, Sophia, and Carlton. She is currently assisting her husband, who is the lead pastor of Wheaton Christian Center.

For booking inquiries or to obtain additional resources or a copy of *Stop the Foolishness for Husbands*, visit _www.paulandfiona.org_.

NOTES

1   June Fuentes, "Tearing Down Our Homes," *A Wise Woman Builds Her Home*, April 29, 2008, https://proverbs14verse1.blogspot.com/2008/04/tearing-down-our-homes.html.

2   Eunor Guti, *Wise Woman* (Harare, Zimbabwe: EGEA Publications, 2006).

3   Graça Machel, UN Secretary-General's Expert on the Impact of Armed Conflict on Children, "Impact of Armed Conflict on Children," UNICEF, August 26, 1996, www.unicef.org/graca/a51-306_en.pdf.
    Graça Machel, "Land-mines: A deadly inheritance," UNICEF, www.unicef.org/graca/mines.htm.

4   John Gottman and Nan Silver, *The Seven Principles for Making Marriage Work* (New York: Harmony, 1999).

5   Shannon and Greg Ethridge, *Every Woman's Marriage* (Colorado Springs: WaterBrook Press, 2010), 51, 120.

6   Pew Research Center, "New Economics of Marriage" (2010).

7   Kevin Leman, *The Birth Order Book* (Grand Rapids: Revell, 2015).

8   Shannon and Greg Ethridge, *Every Woman's Marriage*.

9   Emerson Eggerich, *Love and Respect* (Nashville: Thomas Nelson, 2014).

10 Cambridge Dictionary, https://dictionary.cambridge.org/us.

11 Laura Schlessinger, *Ten Stupid Things Couples Do to Mess Up Their Relationships* (New York: Harper Perennial, 2002).

12 Jay Dixit, "You're Driving Me Crazy!: How small irritants become big issues—and what to do about them," *Psychology Today*, March 1, 2009, https://www.psychologytoday.com/us/articles/200903/youre-driving-me-crazy.

13 Tina Ray, "Is Social Networking Destroying Marriages? 5 Tips to Protect Your Partnership," *Covenant Eyes*, March 20, 2012, https://www.covenanteyes.com/2012/03/20/are-social-networking-sites-destroying-your-marriage-5-tips-to-protect-your-partnership/.

14 David Murrow, *What Your Husband Isn't Telling You* (Bloomington, MN: Bethany House Publishers, 2012).

15 Stuart Brody, PhD, and Rui Miguel Costa, PhD, "Sexual Satisfaction and Health Are Positively Associated with Penile-Vaginal Intercourse but Not Other Sexual Activities," *American Journal of Public Health* 102, no. 1 (Jan 2012): 6–7.

16 Laura Schlessinger, *The Proper Care and Feeding of Marriage* (New York: Harper, 2007).

17 Kevin Leman, *7 Things He'll Never Tell You* (Carol Stream, IL: Tyndale House Publishers, 2007), 109.